ANSWERING THE CALL

A PRACTICAL GUIDE FOR ENTERING MUNICIPAL LAW ENFORCEMENT

JON A. DAGGY
WITH
JOSEPH R. THOMPSON

ISBN 10: 0-9818906-0-1
ISBN 13: 978-0-9818906-0-9

Published by Blue Guardian Publishing
5252 Brianna Lane Suite 101
Indianapolis, IN 46235

Copies may be ordered from www.blueguardianpublishing.com

Design by Brian Rodgers Jr. Copyright 2009

Printed by SelfPublishing.com
Printed in the United States of America

Contents

This book is dedicated to the memory of

Thomas A. Walenga

for loyalty and for living an honorable life!

The essence of America lies not in the headlined heroes, but in everyday folks who live and die unknown, yet leave their dreams as legacies.

—Alan Lomax

Foreword

IN this book, *Answering the Call,* Jon Daggy with Joe Thompson tell the story of America's police becoming a true and exclusive profession. This is done trough their eyes and experience. It's a viewpoint from behind the badge. Many of the stories that we as police tell each other over the years are blended into a uniquely vivid tapestry of American policing and its march towards professionalism.

We should all be grateful that the opportunity was taken to write this book. By all, I mean young males and females who have not yet reached adulthood and are exploring the future to see what opportunities lay ahead and what shall they do with their life that will make a difference in untold lives. At the same time realizing that it's not for everyone.

I believe it to be a clear game plan for those men and women who feel that policing is the life for them. This writing goes into great detail as to what you must do to prepare for the trip. Those approaching it as just another job may not have the dedication that it takes to enter this profession. This in no way makes them a failure but only makes it crystal clear that this profession is not for everyone, and their future lies elsewhere.

One group that should be pleased that Sergeant Daggy put this project to pen and ink is veteran police officers. I can say this with conviction because I am a very senior member of this profession. Starting in the Military Police at the age of eighteen, I am now approaching 50 years in law enforcement service. As I race towards the twilight of my career, and as I read this book, mind raced back to different times when my hair was dark and there was more of it, I asked myself, "How did I get into this business?" Do I feel now as I did then? Yes and this writing assured me that I did the right thing with my life. I believe it will have the same effect on other veteran Officers.

Another group is all adult citizens who get the opportunity to see how professional police officers are formed and how these same Officers view them. I think it will drive home to this group that police are real people and not abstract creatures who come from a different place. It should instill confidence and pride in "their" police when they discover to what extent of training and preparation men and women must compete before they achieve the status of police officer. I imagine that it will surprise some with what police are also surprised, angered, and pleased with when it comes to citizen contact. I can almost hear the refrains of, "I could not do that job," or, "I wish I could live my life over, and I believe that I could have been a good police officer."

This was not written by a scholarly academician who observed the actions of police. It was not written by someone who was limited by relying on interviews. Nor was it written by someone who was unfamiliar with police terminology and never experienced their gut tighten when the radio barked their call number or when they had to go through a door first. No, it was written by a police officer who has experienced these things and worked with other men and women who share these feelings and experiences. It was written by an Officer that came from a long line of professional police officers.

For sure this is not the only way police work can be studied; it's just the best way.

This should be required reading for all adult American citizens. Maybe then, just maybe, we would have a better citizenry.

Thanks for taking the time
and effort to write this book.

—Captain E. Tim Foley
Indianapolis, Indiana
September 2008

ACKNOWLEDGEMENTS

ONE thing that is quickly learned in writing a book is that it's never done alone. There are many people that influence the decision and have helped greatly along the way whether they realized it or not.

Many thanks go to:

Kyle Hannon
Captain E. Tim Foley Indianapolis Metropolitan Police Department
Chief Leo A. Daggy Ret. Mishawaka Police Department
Nancy, Michael, and Bob: Thanks for the inspiration.
Major Forrest E. Morgan Ret. USAF
Priscilla Krege
IPD Vice Unit "The Best of the Best"
Captain Matt Crockett Ret. Indianapolis Police Department
Lieutenant Jerry Barker Ret. Indianapolis Metropolitan Police Department
Sergeant Robert Hoke Ret. Indianapolis Police Department
Officer Mel McNairy Ret. Indianapolis Police Department
Assistant Chief David Chapman Notre Dame Police Department
Brian Rodgers Jr.
Lori Reitz
Officer Sonya Daggy Indianapolis Metropolitan Police Department
Tony Reitz
Christine Edge
Detective John Bolin Indiana Gaming Commission

Detective Commander Ken Kroft Dyer Indiana Police Department
Detective Sergeant Kevin Kinnee Ret. Indianapolis Police Department
Detective Sergeant Steve Smith Indianapolis Metropolitan Police Department
Sergeant Klayton South Ret. USMC
Dr. Natalie Hipple PhD
Brian Viscuso
Dr. Ed McGarrell PhD
Sergeant Mark Brown Indianapolis Metropolitan Police Department
Indianapolis Police Department Training Academy
Sergeant Calvin Banks Ret. U.S. Treasury Police
Officer Angela Davis Phoenix Police Department
Chief Michael Crooke Cumberland Police Department
Polly 33
Sergeant Ian Goldsmith Ret. South Australia Police
Constable Stuart Clough Leicestershire Constabulary, England
Bill Parrish
Captain Joseph Finch Indianapolis Metropolitan Police Department
Captain Brian Nanavaty Indianapolis Metropolitan Police Department
Deputy Chief William Benjamin Indianapolis Metropolitan Police Department
Lieutenant Richard Kivett Indianapolis Metropolitan Police Department
Robert Welch
Sergeant David Rhodes Indiana University Police Department
Detective Michael A. Mitchell Indianapolis Metropolitan Police Department

PURPOSE OF THE BOOK

THIS book is meant to help people with the desire to enter the municipal law enforcement profession. It is not a text book but more of a guide to help those interested along the way to get a positive start to the unique profession of policing. It is composed of thoughts and opinions that come from facts and mistakes that both active and retired Officers have made in the past (including the authors).

No one will have a perfect career. If finding a perfect police department is your goal, the journey is going to be disappointing. Finding the perfect place to work is as practical as finding the perfect school or church. The idea is to make the best of the department that you join, and use your experiences to leave it as a better person and better department.

This book is also not the final word—just a helper. There are many retired Officers that are libraries of knowledge that you should also utilize. Additionally, many college alumni organizations can help find those in the profession willing to guide you in your career decisions.

It should also be understood that each department hires differently, and there are some that hire based on who you know and not what you know. Nevertheless, an honorable and honest career is possible no matter the department. Chapter 1 touches on a Personal Honor Code. This is done since Honor is mentioned throughout the book, and the fact that some academies do not teach the concept of Honor. It is mentioned in oaths and talked about, but never explained in detail. Hopefully this explanation will act as a primer for your code, should you not already have one.

Lastly, there will be those that will dismiss this book, which is their right. Just keep an open mind when reading, and hopefully it will assist you should you decide to answer the call.

Chapter 1

Honor and Your Personal Code

POLICING is a warrior profession. Along with other warrior professions of courage, it's a call to valor. As radical as it sounds, it shouldn't. True warriors have protected right from wrong and fought for justice all through history. Warriors have always lived by a code: an Honor code. In saying this, one does not have to be a member of the military or a police officer to be a warrior. There are many people who train hard as in martial arts or some type of self defense and live life by a personal Honor code. They may go through life never having to defend themselves or their Honor; yet, they are prepared. Also some police officers don't follow any Honor code and don't live life as a warrior even though they are in a warrior profession.

Professional athletes are called warriors by the media; however, most of them have no honor code and do not train for true combat. Firemen may be referred to as warriors since they do train for combat against fire. Many have battled people in the line of their work, and most of them live by an honor code. They are definitely heroes.

Police take an oath when they join the police department, but most don't remember the oath even though it's usually on a signed certificate that's hung on a wall, filed away, or put in a scrap book. This is not a problem if the Officer has a personal Honor code. If a personal Honor code is followed, the oath will be followed.

Police officers make mistakes since they are human. Nobody is perfect, and nobody is a saint. They are hard working humans doing a very challenging and rewarding job. If a police officer follows a personal honor code, he will likely make fewer mistakes since his intention will always be the correct or Honorable one. When done properly there is no more honorable profession than police work. Not many other professions require a person to wear body armor, carry a gun, and solve other people's problems on a daily basis.

Colonel Forrest E. Morgan (a retired Major in the United States Air Force and a martial artist) states that honor is made up of three basic tenets; Obligation, Justice, and Courage (Morgan, 142).

Obligation is answering the call to serve. As a police officer you have many obligations. First is an obligation to your self to do the right thing. Second is your obligation to make it home safe to your other obligation— your family. There's an obligation to the community, department, and the country. Police are the first line soldiers in the war on domestic terrorism. It is that huge, very serious commitment that police make when they decide to go into the warrior profession. Officers should avoid being obligated to dishonorable people. These are people such as part-time employers that will pay an Officer well; however, want the Officer to look the other way for "minor things" such as gambling. Never shall I do anything to dishonor myself, my teammates, my department, or my country!

Justice simply means to know the difference between right and wrong (Morgan, 144). This can include making the right decision over the popular one. Police have to make decisions in a split second or at least in a short amount of time. The responsibility of justice is an awesome one. Police fight for overall justice by enforcing the law fairly, equally, with impartiality. However, as humans, Officers sometimes lose sight when it's time to see justice done. This happens at the hands of a small number of corrupt Officers that tarnish the profession and they ultimately get discovered. Most police officers do the right thing. You never hear about it because it's the few that cover up wrong doings that make the news. They don't stand for justice and obviously have no personal Honor code.

Courage is being brave and facing the danger involved with the job. It does not mean there will be no fear. Moral courage is the fortitude to do what is right, no matter what the personal cost (Morgan, 148). This goes along with justice and doing the right thing for the right reasons.

Coming into the profession with a personal Honor code is great mentally to start with. It is never too late to start following a personal Honor code. Hopefully, a personal honor code will be established and prevent bad something bad from happening via a bad choice. A personal Honor code is stronger than any oath a police officer will take since it comes from the Officer's heart.

References
Morgan, F. E. Living the Martial Way. Fort Lee, New Jersey: Barricade Books Inc., 1992.

Chapter 2

The Police Warrior

BEFORE entering the police profession, one should develop a warrior mindset. There are police officers that still don't understand or have this mindset, and many recruits leave the academy without developing it. This is where the "Thin Blue Line" actually starts and where true guts are made.

People in society can be broken into three separate groups; Sheep (people), Wolves (the criminals), and Sheep Dogs which are the protectors (Grossman, 2004). In this setting, they are the police officer warrior.

People do not always appreciate the police until they need them. A true warrior acknowledges this but will still do his job of protecting society from the deviants that prey on people. At times the police officer warrior's job will necessitate violence. If a person has no capacity for violence, then he should not become a police officer; rather, they should stay in society and allow the police to do the job without casting judgment.

Even the most liberal of people that do not care for the police warriors will change their attitude should they become a victim of violence. They will want something done *pronto.* Ironically, even if their situation is resolved, they will go back to not accepting or respecting the police warrior. They live in denial and believe that as along as nothing is happening to them; criminals should be treated as misled individuals who are committing crimes for being "wronged" in life. They look at the police with more disdain than they do the criminals until they are the prey. These are the same type of people that know that a tragic event happened on September 11, 2001 but want to continue to live in a September 10, 2001 world.

As a police officer warrior, it is not easy to keep an open mind with people that think the way of the sheep, but the true warrior does not worry about negative perceptions against him and his fellow warriors, he does the job he was called to do. He protects the flock to the best of his ability since he can not be everywhere at once. Crime will always exist, but the police officer warriors that work every hour, every day, and every night keep total anarchy from happening. No matter how technologically advanced society becomes, the human element will always be involved in the protection of citizens. There will always be a need for the police officer warrior, and he will always show up and take care of business even if that entails using violence against a violent predator. The attitude of the warrior with an honorable mission and the commitment to serve people is what separates his use of violence from unacceptable uses of violence from the criminal predator. The true police officer warrior uses violence as a tool to stop the predator. He never uses it to punish.

WHICH ARE YOU?

Do you hold a capacity for violence? If you had to, could you pull a trigger to stop another violent person? If you hesitate and wait for things to happen without knowing if you have the capacity to stop violence with violence, you're going to be too late and possibly hurt. There's no shame if you don't have this capacity, but policing is not the occupation for you. If you accept the fact that even symbolically, you are the protector of society and the true first line of defense in society; then, you may have what it takes to become a police officer warrior. Knowing before entering the profession will save a lot of heartache and tax dollars later. Only you can look in the mirror and honestly accept the fact that you have or don't have the inner strength to become the police officer warrior.

References
Grossman, D. and Christensen, L.W. On Combat: The Psychology and Physiology of Deadly Conflict in War and in Peace. Illinois: PPCT Research Publications, 2004.

Chapter 3

The Calling

PEOPLE enter the police profession for many different reasons. Many Officers are second, third, even fourth generation police officers. These Officers are following in the footsteps of their parents and actually feel they have a calling. Some are going to realize that after they serve this country in the military, they'll want to return home and continue serving on a smaller, more intimate scale. Others are getting out of college and need a job. The reasons people choose to go into police work are as diverse as the police community is now.

Officers that are "born" into police work by having one or both parents that are officers are simply talking on a profession that they feel is their legacy. Like any other profession, one or more of the children will follow in their parent's footsteps. Many of these officers will, after graduating from high school, enter the military, college, or both. After all, they have to burn a couple of years since most departments will not appoint you until you are at least 21 years of age. Some have argued that age 25 would be a more mature age to enter law enforcement, but that's debatable. This type of officer may bring knowledge of what it's like to grow up in a police family. A police family is where one or both parents are a police officer. They will have limited knowledge of how the job is done since most police do not go home and talk about what has happened during the shift with their family. Most of the information would be inappropriate for children to hear anyway.

The individual that comes from a police family will ultimately give a hint or let the police parent know their intention of joining the force. The police parent will nearly always try to talk the youth into another profession. Like most kids, he will probably act as if he understands his parent, do what he wants, and join the police department.

These officers don't go through as much culture shock one may get after entering the profession. Still they do not know the job and need to go through training and learn to be the police just like everybody else.

Most departments still only require a high school diploma to be hired as a police officer; although, more are requiring at least some college. At one point they would even higher an 18 year old. This was most likely to reflect the military. Policing is a "Quasi Military" institution, but more on that later. After high school, unless you're a lazy dead-beat, you are going to either get a job, got to college, or enter the military. You're searching for that quality time between 18 and 21 years of age to do something educational and constructive. The dead-beat can stay away from policing. If you're not self motivated and do not like to work, you're going to be an even less motivated police officer. Stay at home and let somebody that really wants to do the job have your spot.

The military is a great starting point for any young man or woman no matter what they later choose to do in life. Many a police officer served his country in the military and continued serving after being discharged. Police are the first line of defense since they work 24 hours a day, seven days a week, and 365 days a year. The military veteran, if he's an honorable person will make an outstanding officer.

These officers usually make it through the academy with no problem since they have already been through boot camp or basic training. At first, they may not write reports and document as well as their college counterparts, but they can adapt and catch on. Due to the fact that they served in the military, they usually have a sharp uniform and appear squared away and are very organized and neat. Many of them live their life like this and make great employees.

If military veteran police officer is not adaptable, he will have a difficult time adjusting to the nature of police work. Police work involves working in a gray area of decision making and discretion. In the military, things are defined as right or wrong or black and white. It's admirable to want to lock up everybody that breaks the law; however, there is not enough police or time in a day to do this, which is why police are given the power of discretion. Discretion is a power. Not adapting can be a cause of frustration and will ultimately embitter the officer.

As in every profession, there are individuals that learn to work the system to benefit them while doing little or nothing to contribute to the occupation or community. The military and police both have these types of individuals. When this person leaves the military with this mindset about how to work the government, he brings this with him to the institution of police work. If this employee is left un-checked early on, he will work the system without contributing very much to it.

Many departments pay a yearly incentive if an officer receives a college degree. Usually this only tops out with a four year degree. During the 1970's there was a big push by the federal government to help police officers by granting and loaning officers' money to get a college degree. It was called the Law Enforcement Education Program (LEEP) and was established in 1968 by the Omnibus Crime Control and Safe Streets Act. This LEEP program not only helped pay for four year degrees but also graduate and PhDs. Some Officers even got a law degree under this program. It was discontinued allegedly due to mismanagement of the funds and many other problems.

College incentive programs have helped get more college educated people into the police profession. Of course when these programs started during the 1980's college educated rookie police officers had to deal with harassment and prejudices from veteran officers who did not go to college.

Admittedly, just because a person went to college and got a degree, will not make one a good police officer. However, the life experience of living in a diverse college community will help prepare a person to accept different cultures, ethnicities, and race if he has developed an open mind. Also, especially if you went away to college, you have to produce by passing or you get kicked out of college. This helps develop a work mentality that can bring a positive quality to any job.

Former college students tend to write very good reports and have little difficulty with the academic part of academy training. Conversely, the military veteran most of the time eases through the physical training routines in the academy.

There's a philosophy out there that you have to "come from the streets to understand the streets." It's a belief that you will not make a good police officer if have grown up in the country or a small town; thus, potentially having little interaction and experience with people of other races. You may have some learning to do should you enter the profession. However, if you keep an open mind, you will learn the streets and understand those cultures that are different than yours. There are police officers that have come from the "streets" and had terrible instincts and made poor police officers. Great police officers come from every part of this country; and, as mentioned before, they are a reflection of the community it serves. That includes the national community. It will be up to you, as a police officer, to either help make it a better community or just be another body wearing a uniform. Hopefully you can become a Professional American Police Officer.

APPLYING TO THE POLICE DEPARTMENT

There will be more on fitness later in the book, and hopefully you practice it as part of your daily life. If you don't, now would be a good time to begin a running and weight lifting regimen. Push-ups and abdominal crunches should be incorporated into whatever fitness program you utilize. You'll thank yourself later...

After you've made the decision to enter one of the greatest professions, you have to make the initial step of applying to become a police officer. There are about as many different application processes as there are police departments in the country. Still, this is where a prospective officer must start preparing himself by thinking and acting as if he's going to become a police officer. If you are a male and you still have that long hair, or different "style of the month" that was totally cool in college, time to get it cut. Police officers have conservative hair cuts. If you really don't understand what that means, you can call the department and ask them what the policy is on the uniform officer's haircut. Some applicants have it cut as if they just came out of military boot camp. That is fine but is does not have to be that sharp.

Before you make the trek to the department or government location where you apply, in addition to the haircut, you need to dress appropriately. Remember, if you are serious, you want to leave that impression. Unless told otherwise, wear business casual clothes. There will be later times when a suit is appropriate. The idea is to start acting and looking professional. If you haven't already incorporated these into your life, start using the phrases "Yes Sir" and "Yes Ma'am". When you get to the department or place of application you will almost always be greeted by a city employee. If you are greeted by anybody whether civilian or a sworn police officer, stand up straight, look them in the eye, and give a strong handshake. A strong handshake shows exactly what it implies, strength. It also shows confidence and tells the person whom you are greeting that you are genuine about why you are there.

You may not be given an application on this first step. This may be just one of many steps. After all, it is government and by nature bureaucratic. You may simply have to sign up with some personal information. They may also take your finger prints to see if you have a criminal record. Yes, as stupid as it may seem, they have caught criminals and people with warrants this way. They will also use your personal information to see if you have an arrest record and what kind of driving record you have. Later, if you make it to this point, they may check your name in police reports. You will be competing against what could be thousands of other applicants, and if you have a lot of interaction with the police even with no arrests, it could set off a red flag.

During this early part of the process, you will be given an application to fill out. Since typewriters are nearly obsolete, you will probably have to do this freehand unless they offer on on-line or electronic version of it. If it's an application that you have to fill out by hand, pre-write your answers before you put them in the blanks of the application. Since your future employers are looking for professionals, you want this application to be as neat as possible. If your penmanship is not very neat, get a friend or relative to fill those blanks in for you—unless it states that you must fill it out yourself. Everything is a test, especially this early in the game.

Lastly, be honest in your application. Once again your honor will be questioned if the police department finds out you were dishonest on your application. Police are good at finding out the truth and reading through lies whether in person or on paper. Credibility starts here in police work and should never be abandoned for the rest of your career and life.

THE INTERVIEW

When your application gets accepted, the next likely step will be an interview. If you don't get to this step and receive a denial letter from the department, don't fret, there are many great officers that tried for the department up to five times before they finally were accepted. Patience truly is a virtue if you are passionate about entering the police profession. Nothing happens fast. The police have adopted a military saying of, "Hurry up and wait." This is one of the bureaucratic truths of this fine profession that will never go away. Additionally, rushing the procedure of hiring a new officer would lend itself to potential mistakes and rushed judgments.

There are many ways to prepare for an interview. One is to simply research business books that explain how to handle your self during an interview. One such book is *Sweaty Palms: The Neglected Art of Being Interviewed* by H. Anthony Medley. Another book is *101 Great Answers to the Toughest Interview Questions* by Ronald Frye. Regardless, the police interview is going to be different from most other interviews—including a military interview.

Again the style of dress is important. Whether you are a male or female, a dark business suit should be worn for the interview. Conservative dress is expected. Men should be clean shaven with a short hair cut (as mentioned before).

Women should have the hair up in a bun. Shoes should be shined, and a gloss would even be better. There is a good chance that one or more of the police members of the board will have been in the military, and they will certainly be judging your appearance. The impression of appearing as a police officer will show the board you are serious about the interview and the career.

The board usually consists of four to five uniformed, seasoned police officers from patrolman to Lieutenant. If they show any emotion during the interview, it would be very unusual. They want to treat everybody the same and not show favoritism.

When you are brought into the interview room, there will be a place for you to sit down. Wait until being told to sit before doing so. Sit with both feet flat on the floor pointing forward and hands should be on the table on front of you. The officers will start reading you immediately as you enter the room—another reason why you should be well dressed. First impressions are very important. A ranking officer will welcome you, introduce each of the board members, and explain the rules of the interview. As they speak, maintain eye contact and acknowledge him or her with "Yes Sir"' or "Yes Ma'am." As he introduces the board members, greet each of them with your eyes and a nod.

There will be a time limit for the interview. Since your hands are already sitting on the table or just in front of you, take a glance at your watch and note your time. Most sessions will be 20 to 25 minutes with an average of six questions. If you keep your answers to about three minutes a question, you will be managing your time well. Each question will have "anchors" or "answers" in which they will be expecting. There can be *high anchors* and *low anchors.* The *high* anchors are worth more points obviously than the *low* anchors. They may even allow for an answer that they didn't have as an anchor.

Anchors are an attempt to keep interviews fair and equal for interviewees. If the board members are writing a lot while you are answering, you are hitting anchors. There is that occasional board member that waits until they are finished and will fill in his answers when you are out of the room.

If, during the interview, you feel you answer poorly and are on to the next question. Take a deep breath and think of the next question as a clean slate. That may just be a tough question that everybody is having difficulty with. Also just because you may have given the answer in a previous question and think you may be repeating yourself, go ahead and repeat yourself. The new question has a whole new set of anchors, and you still have to hit them for interview points. Think of each question as its own entity, and you have about three minutes to fill it. When you feel you are finished with the question, you can pause and let the board guess that you are finished or say "Thank you," and that will let the board know you are ready for the next question and save you valuable interview time.

The questions that you may be asked will be picked by the department. A few questions may be unique to the department or to police nationally that is a hot topic at the moment. These might include racial issues, police corruption, or simply breaking the law. If you keep up on current events and watch the news, you will get a good idea of the type of unique question they might ask. Still no matter which department is giving the interview, there are going to be basic questions in one form or another that will always be asked.

> *Why do you want to be a police officer? What have you done to prepare yourself for the profession of a police officer? What qualifications or skills do you possess that will make you assist you should you become a police officer? What do*

you expect from the police department? How do you handle stress?

The first question that is asked is, "why you want to be a police officer?" The textbook answer, and one that the police have heard for the last century, is that you want to help people. Believe me—they are sick and tired of this answer. You can help people by bagging their groceries. Good answers include the fact that there is a lot of freedom with the job. You get to work with a diverse group of people. You get to perform a service for the local community. It fills you with pride to be able to do a unique job that not everybody can do.

The next question is, "how did you prepare yourself?" You can start with things such as your major in college, or your service in the military. Perhaps you were in the Military Police. Maybe you did some security work. Many departments offer a ride along program, and you may have participated in that and interviewed the officer. There are many books to read and publications on this subject. Maybe you spoke to a relative that was in the profession. Also, they want to know how you prepared yourself physically. Did you take a self-defense class? (Be careful with this one and do not brag about how many black belts you have. Just touch on the fact that you have taken one. Humility goes along way in martial arts and police work.)

The qualifications or skills question is really the time to brag about yourself and accomplishments without coming across as arrogant. Simply tell the board that it's not easy for you to talk about yourself and then talk about yourself! This is especially true with the skills and qualifications question. This is where you bring your experience in and may even repeat what you have answered in the question about preparing yourself. You may have previous law enforcement experience. Maybe you obtained a law degree or majored in pre-law or Criminal Justice in college. Were you a part of a work/study program in college such as the SPEA (School of Public and Environmental Affairs)? Indiana University offers this program, in which one becomes a police officer on a college campus and has to deal with your peers. This is very powerful training, and it turns out excellent police officers. When you were in college, did you work as a Resident Assistant and have to confront peers with rule violations and document them? Were you an intern? Have you volunteered for law enforcement events such as traffic control? Were you a security guard and had to deal with people and handle problems to keep the police from being called to the company that employed you? Did you sit on a suicide hot line where you learned to talk people out of making a terrible choice? Did you work in corrections? These are all valuable experiences to document in the interview and application process.

One of the tougher questions for applicants is, "What do you expect from the department?" A decent answer is that you expect to be trained well and supported—as long as you do the right thing. You expect the department to be an honorable institution and truly stand for justice. You expect your co-workers and supervisors to be loyal, honorable, and trustworthy. You expect to be kept up to date with changes in the law and city ordinances. Lastly, you expect the police department to continue to be the professional organization that it has a reputation for. You may add that you will uphold that reputation as an employee.

The last question is, "How do you handle stress?" The most likely answers to that question will be exercise, hobbies, meditation, praying, attending church, community events. Doing family events that help take your mind off what is causing the stress may be another answer. It's a personal question but it's important for the interview board to know that you have a safeguard in place already before entering a stressful job.

There will probably be more questions and possibly a writing assignment. It's never too late to learn to write, and, once again, there are many resources to help you with writing styles. The best way to do well on a writing assignment is to keep things simple. This means try not to write big words that neither you nor the officer reading it knows, and get to the point. Police reports should be very simply written. This does not mean you can not be detailed when writing—just keep it simple. The topic could be anything—a question about race, corruption, or why laws need to be enforced. They will look at your grammar and sentence structure. More and more officers have attended college and were scrutinized for four years on their writing, so expect some scrutiny.

If there is anything to truly learn from this chapter, it is to prepare yourself. As you've read, there are many ways to prepare. Have your friends make up a mock interview board and practice these and any other type of employment questions. The more you practice, the more you will answer the questions automatically cutting down on the interview stress. Don't forget your own life experiences. Are you a parent, do you have children? Being a parent is one of the most difficult and responsible jobs you will ever experience. Have you had an experience that may or may not have included a positive interaction with the police? If you had a negative interaction, that should be kept to yourself during an interview. Police officers hear negativity towards them all the time, and there's no quicker way to turn off an adult's listening than to criticize him and the career he or she chose. If you have had a negative experience with a police officer in life, use that memory to better yourself as a police officer if you get accepted into one of the world's greatest professions. Also, after you become a police officer, find out why that was a negative experience. Be open minded and honest with yourself, and see if it wasn't something that was actually caused by you, then move on.

Chapter 4

The Academy Game

BEING ACCEPTED

CONGRATULATIONS, you passed the multitude of tests and got an offer to become an Officer. Chances are you have been poked and prodded by a doctor, gone through a physical and psychological test, spoke to a psychologist, and even passed a polygraph test. Even if you are one of those people that think you can pass a polygraph by lying, remember trained police officers will be giving you the test. Just be honest and answer truthfully. Even if your deception doesn't show, a seasoned cop can read you. There is a belief that it is up to the polygraph examiner as to whether you pass it or not, so be honest and don't take any chances.

Chances are you will be given a date to show up to the academy. It may be a long or short time gap. During this wait, a range of emotions ranging from fear to excitement may be felt in anticipation of your first day. Questioning the decision to go into law enforcement may also enter your mind. These feelings are natural and do not mean the right or wrong decision was made. Nevertheless, you should have physically started preparing yourself long before being accepted. Consider yourself warned. You will regret not being prepared physically. Start now and continue for the rest of your life, this is one way to keep yourself alive. You will be given every opportunity to succeed, but only you can do the work. Regardless of family history, race, education, or how much money you have; the academy is a bridge you must cross alone. Are you really ready for the challenge?

Before entering the academy, you should mentally prepare yourself by thinking of the academy as a very serious game that you have to play in order to become a police officer. The academy is going to be overwhelming with not only physical tests—academic tests also play a big part in the experience. Professional police instructors have an awesome responsibility; not only to you and your families, but also to the other Officers on the department and to the community. The instructors will seem impatient and yell a lot. None of this is intended to be personal. They are concerned with helping build you into the best police officer possible as well as teaching you how to stay alive on the streets. Be mentally prepared. Think of it as a quasi-military version of boot camp emphasizing law enforcement instead of warfare.

TRAINING STARTS

On the date you show up the academy, you will be doing most of your activities in a suit. Make a good impression and come appropriately dressed. Even on this day if one person messes up, the whole group will have to do push-ups. This is not to punish everybody; this is where the actual team building starts. Unless told otherwise, when a person is told to do push-ups, everybody should be doing them and showing the academy staff they are becoming a team. Evaluations are not only done on paper but they are locked away in your instructors' memories. Earning a reputation starts on day ONE! Where it goes after that is up to the individual recruit.

On the first day you will be given books, miscellaneous

equipment, probably assigned a room or a locker depending on whether or not it is a live-in Academy. The first part of the day will most likely involve you getting sworn in or taking an oath. You might get your picture taken with the Chief, Mayor, or Sheriff. You will also probably have to fill out forms and paperwork regarding your tax deductions and health insurance. It can be a little overwhelming. Take a deep breath; these are important documents you are signing, if you are not sure, ask. At some point on the first day you will meet the Academy staff. Some academies call them instructors, some call them counselors. You should simply listen to them and call them "Sir" or "Ma'am". One of the instructors will probably be the one most responsible for the class. Think of him or her as the class coordinator or senior drill instructor. The staff will tell you that everything you have done in life and accomplished will mean little during your tenure at the Academy. At this point, everybody is equal and all they are concerned with is the accomplishment of state requirements to build each recruit into a police officer. One piece of advice—be a quiet professional about your skill or accomplishments. If you are as good as you think you are, you will get noticed for the right reasons, not because you are a loud mouth who talks too much.

The police department has already invested time and money into the recruit before he or she even arrives on day one. The instructors are also under pressure to produce the best police officers possible. There may be civilian instructors and retired police officers as civilian instructors. Civilian instructors tend to get a negative reputation since they are not the "real police." This is a false assumption, and they know much more about policing than the recruit does in most instances. Nevertheless, they are passionate about building good police officers and deserve respect. After all, they live in the community that the recruit will ultimately be working; therefore, they also have an investment in the recruit. There are things that can't be taught in an academy atmosphere, but academy training is important and is the best place to begin.

Hopefully, in the first days of the academy, the practice of honor, loyalty, respect, and duty will be explained. Nevertheless, this is where the practice starts with the staff and fellow recruits. Police officers personalities do not always mesh. This is also present in the academy where recruits may have personality conflicts with each other and the staff. This is where loyalty kicks in again. You don't have to like the person you work with; however, you still will depend on each other and be there when help is needed. Put another way, you do not have to be best friends, but you have to work together.

The recruit officer will be taught the concept and the rule of the chain of command. It's actually a chain of communication. As in the military, you report to the supervisor above you, and he passes the information up the chain through his supervisor and so forth up to the Chief of Police if it needs to make it that far. This can be done verbally or in writing. The recruit is the bottom of the chain. His supervisor may actually be another officer that is an instructor at the academy but has not attained any rank. When the recruit leaves the academy, his first supervisor will be his field training officer. This concept of reporting to the immediate supervisor is taken too lightly in police work and is violated all the time by officers. Most of the time, this violation occurs with no punitive consequences. Unfortunately, higher-ranking supervisors allow this to happen and it distorts the chain of communication. A common problem with any organization is lack of communication. When the chain of command is broken, a supervisor gets neglected from the communication process, and time is wasted because the chain has to reverse itself to inform the supervisor that should have been included. The only times a person may truly subvert the chain of command is if the immediate supervisor is asking or ordering the subordinate to do something illegal or unethical. The chain may also be broken if a supervisor other than the immediate supervisor is present on a scene and an answer may be needed immediately due to the circumstances at the moment. The supervisor present may be referred to in your report. The chain can not be subverted if your supervisor hurt your feelings because he counseled you for a problem he feels you are having that needs to be remedied.

Everybody in every day life has to deal with stress. Stress is actually healthy because it can prepare and condition a person for times of higher stress. The academy staff will put recruits through very stressful situations and scenarios. This is includes exercise-induced stress. The staff is not going to hit you, but they will use many techniques to "motivate" you. This is all to get you to perform at your highest level. This is to see how well a recruit can handle himself and to prepare the recruit for the street. There will even be a class given about stress management. If a recruit can not handle stress under these controlled situations, he will not be able to handle the street and the wide variety of stressful situations he will encounter over his career. Some people perform very well under stress, some fold up like a card table. Into which category do you fit?

FITNESS

Fitness, as mentioned earlier, should have already started. You probably had to pass a physical agility test to be accepted. Some departments will send a note along with the acceptance letter from the academy to tell the new recruit to start exercising. Please understand, exercise in the academy is not really to get you in shape, it is to get you in better shape. If you are not in shape, it is because you did not want it bad enough, and there is a good chance you will fail the academy as a whole—not just the fitness portion. When you practice push-ups or sit-ups, make sure you use good, proper form. You may be able to do 50 push-ups but if the form is bad, they will not count. There will be team runs to not only promote fitness but also unity within the group. These class formations or squad runs will usually involve some form of cadence and running in step with your fellow recruits. Also, one of you will be given a place of honor and responsible for carrying the class colors. The class colors are usually referred to as the Guidon and Burgee.

Working on hand and forearm strength is a must. Some academy recruits have problems pulling the trigger on the gun when they get to the firearms training portion. Buy a set of hand grips from a sporting goods store. They are rather inexpensive. If you can not afford them, use a couple of old tennis balls and while you are watching television, squeeze until you have exhausted your hands and forearms. If you do this several times a day when you get a break from work, you will develop strength. Simply putting your hands in front of you and opening and closing your fists will develop strength in both the hands and forearms. You are going to have to put your hands on people later to control them. A strong grip is essential.

The following are just some suggestions of exercises that can benefit you prior to starting the Academy. These workouts are designed for two categories of people:

1. *Category I* is for those that have never (or have not recently) been on a routine physical training program.

2. *Category II* is designed for high school and college athletes or military folks that have had routine physical training programs. Usually athletes in sports that require a high level of cardiovascular activity are in Category II. Swimming, running, basketball, soccer and wrestling are good examples of such sports.

WORKOUT FOR CATEGORY I

RUNNING: The majority of the physical activities you will be required to perform during your six months of training at the Academy will involve some form of running. The intense amount of running can lead to overstress injuries of the lower extremities in trainees who arrive not physically prepared to handle the activities. Swimming, bicycling, and lifting weights will prepare you for some of the activities, but ONLY running can prepare your lower extremities for the majority of the activities.

The goal of the category I student is to work up to 16 miles per week of running. After you have achieved that goal, then and only then should you continue on to the category II goal of 30 miles per week. Let me remind you that category I is a nine-week build up program. Follow the workout as best you can and you will be amazed at the progress you will make.

CATEGORY I

RUNNING SCHEDULE I	
WEEKS 1-2:	2 miles/day, about a 10-minute pace, M/W/F (6 miles/week)
WEEK 3:	Some form of Cross training (cycling, swimming, Elliptical machine, yoga/Pilates)
WEEK 4:	3 miles/day, M/W/F (9 miles/wk)
WEEKS 5-6:	2/3/4/2 miles, M / Tu / Th / F (11 miles/wk)
WEEKS 7-8:	3/4/5/2 miles, M / Tu / Th / F (16 miles/wk)
WEEK 9:	same as #7, 8 (16 miles/wk)
* Note: For best results, alternate exercises. Do a set of pushups, then a set of sit-ups, followed by a set of pull-ups, immediately with no rest.	

CATEGORY II

Category II is a more intense workout designed for those who have been involved with a routine physical training schedule or those who have completed the requirements of category I.

DO NOT ATTEMPT THIS WORKOUT SCHEDULE UNLESS YOU CAN COMPLETE THE WEEK #9 LEVEL OF CATEGORY I WORKOUTS

RUNNING SCHEDULE II (M/ Tu / Th / F / Sat) TOTAL	
SETS OF REPETITIONS PROPER FORM on EACH	
WEEKS 1-2:	(3/5/4/5/2) miles 19 miles/week (about an 8-minute pace)
WEEKS 3-4:	(4/5/6/4/3) miles 22 miles/week
WEEK 5:	(5/5/6/4/4) miles 24 miles/week
WEEK 6:	(5/6/6/6/4) miles 27 miles/week
WEEK 7:	(6/6/6/6/6) miles 30 miles/week
*Note: For weeks 8-9 and beyond, it is not necessary to increase the distance of the runs; work on the speed of your 6-mile runs and try to get them down to 7:30 per mile or lower. Rarely would you ever run more than 6 miles while in the Academy. If you wish to increase the distance of your runs, do it gradually: no more than one mile per day increase for every week beyond week 9.	

PT SCHEDULE II (Mon/Wed/Fri)	
SETS OF REPETITIONS	
WEEK 1-2:	6 X 30 PUSHUPS 6 X 35 SITUPS 3 X 10 PULLUPS 3 X 20 DIPS
WEEK 3-4:	10 X 20 PUSHUPS 10 X 25 SITUPS 4 X 10 PULLUPS 10 X 15 DIPS
WEEK 5:	15 X 20 PUSHUPS 15 X 25 SITUPS 4 X 12 PULLUPS 15 X 15 DIPS
WEEK 6:	20 X 20 PUSHUPS 25 X 25 SITUPS 5 X 12 PULLUPS 20 X 15 DIPS
*Note: For weeks 8-9 and beyond, it is not necessary to increase the distance of the runs; work on the speed of your 6-mile runs and try to get them down to 7:30 per mile or lower. Rarely would you ever run more than 6 miles while in the Academy. If you wish to increase the distance of your runs, do it gradually: no more than one mile per day increase for every week beyond week 9.	

These workouts are designed for long-distance muscle endurance. Muscle fatigue will gradually take a longer and longer time to develop doing high repetition workouts. For best results, alternate exercises each set, in order to rest that muscle group for a short time. The above exercises can get a bit boring after a while. Here are some more workouts you can use to break up the monotony.

(#pull-ups) SITUPS:	3, 6, 9, 12, 15, 12, 9, 6, 3
(3x #pull-ups) DIPS:	same as pushups

The only easy day was yesterday! It's up to you to do the work…

DEFENSIVE TACTICS

For the purposes of this book, defensive tactics will refer to any type of training you will receive in the academy to defend yourself or someone else. It will also include deadly force and the use of firearms. Also it includes tactics on how to control a person who is resisting arrest.

In the academy, the recruit will receive training on how to effectively strike and control a person when the level of force the other person is using warrants it. Most police defensive tactics systems today are based on the **Pressure Point Control Tactics** (PPCT) system. One notable person that helped develop this system is Dr. Paul Whitesell who, at the writing of this book, is currently the Superintendent for the Indiana State Police. This system employs basic strikes and kicks and control techniques—including pressure points. This system is only the basics, and will not make you a martial arts superstar. Like everything else, this has to be practiced after the academy to become proficient at it. Defensive tactics are taught to relieve the department of liability in case they aren't used properly on an individual. Basically, if you don't use them correctly, you may be punished both civilly and criminally.

The recruit will learn how to use his open had to strike. This is a very effective technique especially if having to stun a person in the head area. Truthfully, most police officers, even martial artists do not know how to hit with a proper fist. On the street, if a police officer punches a person in the head when justified, he usually breaks the hand and/or injures the fist. Hard techniques, such as the fist if used, are for soft areas of the body like the stomach area. Soft techniques, which are very effective, are used for hard places such as the head or breast area. Just remember, "Hard on soft, soft on hard." Strong techniques combined with loud verbal commands such as "Get back!" or "Get down!" should be loud enough that the whole neighborhood will hear it when applied in a street situation. Follow this up with an arrest technique if the situation calls for an arrest.

In the early 1990's, The Ultimate Fighting Championship appeared on the scene. It is now called Mixed Martial Arts (MMA) since it encompasses both stand-up fighting (punching and kicking) and ground fighting (Jujitsu and wrestling). A small Jujutsu martial artist from Brazil named Royce Gracie was beating fighters much bigger than him by making them comply with his ground fighting holds. Ground fighting became popular overnight and so did MMA. Since more civilians are going to the ground to fight, many police departments have developed ground fighting programs. Now recruits in the academy wear themselves out by learning to defend themselves on the ground. Like anything though, a good program is balanced. Therefore a good Defensive tactics program balances stand-up fighting with ground fighting. It is up to the individual recruit to continue his training in these styles after he leaves the academy.

In martial arts, there is a concept called *Mushin.* It is a Japanese term that literally translates to, "mind, no mind." The Japanese warriors called the Samurai understood this concept nearly a thousand years ago. These warriors trained so much with fighting techniques and weapons that they defended themselves without thinking about it. Simply it's developing muscle memory. In every police academy, every recruit has to qualify with a handgun on a basic State mandated course. Unfortunately for some, this is most of the experience they will receive with a firearm. In some larger departments across the United States that have their own academy, the recruits will actually be subjected to combat courses and scenarios involving the sidearm. This is one of the only areas where a recruit actually develops muscle memory for deadly force situations. This is due to the lethality and the seriousness of deadly force. Misuse of force gets police officers in trouble more than anything; therefore, use of deadly force needs to be taught with the utmost sincerity. Still, defeat on the street can mean death. It's deadly serious!

CHAPTER 5

Hitting the Streets

FIELD TRAINING PROGRAM

PRIOR to graduating from the Academy, the department will assign a Field Training Officer (FTO) to you. There will be a total of three different officers (at least) with whom you will work. The Field Training Program is the "on the job training" you will receive before being released to full duty either by yourself or with a partner depending on the department. If you're an academic person, think of it as the Academy instruction is the Arts and the FTO program is the Science. Almost all field training programs are modeled after the original 1972 San Jose Police Department Field Training Program.

Usually there is an Officer of rank that will put rookies with a Field Training Officer that he or she feels is compatible with the rookie. Unfortunately this doesn't always happen. For the Field Training Officers, this can be one of the most rewarding experiences of their career. It can also be a very stressful time for the rookie. A good FTO program continues on what the Academy has started by building the police officer. This is no place to "tear" a rookie down. It has already been done in the Academy. The rookie will have to work with and hopefully learn from each FTO. Each FTO is different; they all have their own pet peeves and style of policing. Some put a lot of focus on traffic stops, some on drug arrests, and some on report writing. The FTO is there to help. Learn from each one, and when you are on your own develop a style that works for you. Police work is not one size fits all. However, always remember the three (3) golden rules of policing: Safety first, Common Sense second, and then you do police work!

The rookie will be assigned a primary FTO. When the first rotation is complete they will move on to their second and third rotations of FTO. After the third rotation, the rookie will go back to their primary FTO for the fourth and final rotation. Each time a rookie rotates, it will be a new phase. The rookie will spend approximately 20 working days in each phase. The fifth phase is a solo phase. In each phase the rookie will be evaluated every day minus the observation days in the first phase and only weekly in the fifth phase.

The primary phase is the most important. This phase can make or break the rookie. The rookie is usually scared and nervous in this new environment. It is no longer the sterile academy environment. The rookie may spend up to the first week in this phase observing his veteran FTO do the job. Hopefully the FTO will show the new officer how to stay busy and enjoy the job while taking care of the assigned beat. After the first week, the rookie will be evaluated and do a small percentage of the work. He or she will never forget the first time they make an arrest. Starting in this phase and for the rest of the career, the rookie will be exposed to a variety of ordinary and extraordinary situations. Some rookies in the first phase and even on day one have had deadly force encounters. Welcome to police work.

Working in the primary phase of the FTO program and with the primary FTO, things can get overwhelming. There is so much instruction and paperwork to learn that it may seem difficult if not impossible to take. This is where the rookie also learns to balance law with Standard Operating Procedure. A Standard Operating Procedure (SOP) is a rule set up by a police department on how its officers will handle a specific type of situation. This can also conflict with law. For example, many police departments have a policy or an SOP not to pursue vehicles if the initial crime is not a felony. Even though it's not against the law to pursue a criminal in a vehicle for the lesser misdemeanor crime, it's against the department's policy. This means if the officer decides to not follow the SOP, the department may not back him or her in any civil or criminal proceedings against him should one result.

After the 20 days with the primary FTO, the rookie will go to the Second phase of FTO. During this phase, the rookie will be expected to handle about half of the work load. Basic reports will start to get easy, and during this phase the secondary FTO will expose the rookie to more responsibilities and evaluate him on how he handles himself. The most important item a rookie will be evaluated on in any phase will be officer safety. This is how the rookie holds himself and keeps him and other officers safe. One thing that will always be stressed is to keep your gun side away from and keep bodily distance away from the offender. Four to six feet is a safe gap to keep between you and any offender. Your feet should be about shoulder width apart with your heels at a 90° angle towards each other. The hands should be at waist level ready to react if needed. In martial arts this is called a *hanmi* or combative stance. True warriors employ this stance even after they retire from service since it becomes second nature. For many this can become your natural stance. It can be done so discreetly that people will not know you are in a defensive stance. You should always be prepared for an offensive action against you. Greet and treat everyone professionally but always have a plan to defend yourself against that same individual or individuals.

The second phase is a good time for the rookie to start mentally preparing himself for the type of run he is on while traveling to the run. A good FTO will coach him and quiz him while en route to get him to start this type of thinking. This will help develop mushin of the mind. Mentally rehearsing on the way to a run will help develop responses to the type of situation he will possibly encounter. Start this rehearsal of the run here and never stop for the rest of your career. It will save your life. Even if the run turns out to be un-eventful, the brain will still store the thoughts and bring them out the next time a similar type of run is dispatched.

An example of a mental rehearsal for a "man with a gun" dispatch—after receiving and acknowledging the run, while driving, picture in your mind's eye arriving on the run. Then picture scanning the situation for danger—not just for a person with a gun but any type of danger. When you, in your mind, encounter this person with a gun, draw your weapon and command him as to what to do next. Tell him to drop the gun; however, if he points it at you or someone else, you will use deadly force. This type of mental rehearsal will get faster and occur naturally if the rookie starts early and makes it a part of every run. The only constant of every run is the Officer's safety and how he prepares himself on the way to it. *Keep an open mind on each and every run.*

The third phase of the FTO program has the rookie perform the majority of the work while being evaluated every day. Here he will be taught more the use of discretion. At this point, it will probably have been explained and demonstrated that the rookie will truly have to practice discretion to his field training officer's approval. Even though the rookie is developing his own style, he has to conform to the style of the current FTO. Once again this can be very frustrating since police officers have different styles and after so many weeks in this program, the rookie gets sent to a new FTO with what can be a totally different style. A good practice for the rookie is to take all the good things learned from each of his trainers and use them as guides to develop his own style.

In each phase the rookie will be exposed to more and more stressful situations. As with the mental rehearsal mentioned previously, the rookie should start practicing controlled breathing on the way to the run. The heart will naturally start beating faster on a high priority run, and a rookie can develop tunnel vision. The problem with this is when he arrives on the scene and focuses in on his possible threat, he will not see potentially hazardous things going on around him. Deep controlled breathing will help reduce these "blinders" and bring the officer back to the whole situation. Take a deep breath, break out of the tunnel vision, and expect trouble. Start acting like an officer. Act like you know what you're doing. Hold your head up, keep your back straight, and be proud of yourself. Once again, if this gets practiced early on, it will become natural and automatic. It will save the Officer's life whether he realizes it or not.

The fourth phase of the Field Training Program finds the rookie back with the primary officer from the first rotation. This time around, the primary FTO will see just how much the rookie has learned since he started the training program. The rookie will be doing all the work and still will be getting evaluated every day. The first two weeks of this fourth rotation, the FTO will be in uniform. After the first two weeks, the FTO decides if the rookie is ready for the FTO to come in plain clothes. The reason for this is the FTO acts as more of an observer, only to step in on dangerous or unusual runs. Also the public will approach the uniformed officer and not the plain clothes officer. After the two weeks of plain clothes, the FTO decides if the rookie is ready for the fifth and last solo phase. There is a chance the rookie may be held over if he or the FTO feel the rookie is not ready for the solo phase. Although the rookie may feel that there may be a stigma attached for being held over, one must remember that adults learn differently. This will not keep the rookie from becoming a great police officer if he still has the drive to do so. We all have a different learning curve and different ways of learning.

The final phase of the Field Training Program is the solo phase. The rookie will be evaluated weekly by a supervisor during this phase. This is the first time the rookie will be alone in a vehicle, answering run calls, and doing proactive police work. This is where the rookie truly starts to develop his or her own style. There is a great weight lifted by not having an FTO looking over the rookie's shoulder constantly, but also a great deal of responsibility. The safety net (FTO) is not sitting next to you now. Also the rookie's confidence will grow even more during this phase due to the fact decisions have to be made without immediate oversight. The rookie will be more accepted by the veteran officers and start enjoying the job even more. This is where the responsibility of having personal on-the-job freedom starts. Police officers can either use it or abuse it. A reputation in police work starts early and will follow the officer if he or she leaves it un-checked. Remember, be a Quiet Professional. This is where you start to be that *professional American police officer.*

The book *Tactical Edge* by Charles Remsberg lists positive self-talk that street Officers should practice. These should be written down and read every day before hitting the streets. They are great "auto-suggestions" for your mind and will help keep you alive (Remsberg, 1986). They are as follows:

1. On any high-risk call, I will survive.
2. I have succeeded on dangerous calls before.

3. I know the tactics I need.
4. I know how to make the physical moves I need.
5. I am skilled with my firearms.
6. I can stay focused on what I have to do.
7. I can take care of myself.
8. I have options for controlling any problem.
9. I can take each call step by step, without rushing.
10. I can breathe deeply to control stress any time I start feeling tense.
11. I can keep any situation within limits I can handle.
12. I can decide not to be afraid.
13. I can defeat any threats against me.
14. I can use deadly force to save my life or the life of someone else.
15. I can survive and keep going, no matter what, even if I am hit.

Place these written or typed suggestions somewhere where you can read them every day. A good place is to tape them up on a wall where you put on your uniform before going to work every day. This way the suggestions will start to become as natural as putting on that uniform every day.

During the first year, it's mandatory with some departments that an Officer wears his body armor. While this seems like a no-brainer, there are Officers that believe that if it's their time to go, they are going to die body armor or not. While there may be determinist, religious belief based on that, it won't matter if the Officer takes a bullet in a gun fight and now his partner has to worry about him along with the suspect with whom they are in a shoot-out. Even the Samurai wore armor into battle because it upped their chances of winning. The uniform should feel incomplete when you put it on without a vest. Wear the vest. It gives you an advantage in a gun fight and may even help if the assailant tries to stab you. In 2007, more than one-third of police officers murdered were not wearing body armor and analysts estimate that up to half of all Officers do not wear bullet-resistant vests regularly. (Johnson, 2008)

References

Remsberg, C. The Tactical Edge: Surviving High Risk Patrol. Illinois: Calibre Press, Inc., 1986, 36-37.

Johnson, K. (2008, October 24-26). Officers at risk by resisting armor. USA Today, pp. A1, A2.

Chapter 6

The Assignment

AFTER the rookie has completed the FTO program, he or she will be assigned to certain area of town to run a beat. They never get assigned to a specialized unit as you see on television. That is Hollywood and if that were to happen, the department would be asking for trouble by not letting the Officer get the practical street experience of running a marked police vehicle and answering calls for service in a 911 car. All of the basic skills and talents of a police officer are developed here. A fair amount of time to spend in uniform and running a "beat" car is five years. After five years, the basic skills are developed and will compliment the Officer should he or she decide to become a detective.

During this first year of being assigned, the new Officer will be bounced around to different beats usually running the beat when a veteran officer has a day off. This also depends on the size of the Department. The new officer will not be referred to as a rookie so much anymore even though he or she still is one. The new Officer will be accepted even more but will still be the new person. The good ol' FNG (freaking new guy)! On busy police departments, the veterans Officers are just happy to have the extra bodies out there helping. A good veteran Officer will help the new Officer out with difficult runs. Nobody comes on this job knowing everything and a good veteran Officer remembers how difficult it was that first year. The new Officer will develop a liking to a certain area that he or she gets to cover and hopefully will get to run that beat in the future permanently.

The new Officer will learn the police jargon and also how to balance out proactive and non-proactive work. The first thing the veteran will tell the new Officer is to "take care of your beat." This means no matter what beat you are assigned, you have the responsibility for the reports, accidents, and runs that come out on that beat on the shift you are working. There are times when that will be impossible such as when you are taking a report for a large incident such as a shooting, homicide, rape, etc. Other than those incidents, you have to listen to the radio and take the runs on your beat. This is often difficult for young officers that think they need to stop every car that has a violation. While that is a part of your job, you must balance that with you beat responsibility. It is impossible to arrest every person out there that is committing a crime. On a smaller scale, one could spend the whole shift writing tickets. Everybody makes mistakes when they drive. There are many laws and ordinances out there and once again, it's impossible to enforce all of them. Not everybody needs to go to jail or get a ticket. Choose wisely and you will learn what works and what doesn't and when the right time to enforce them. That is another aspect of discretion to be used prudently.

The new Officer is still on probation during his first year. That is why he or she is still technically a rookie. It is very natural during these first few years to enjoy the job so much that you can't wait for your days off to end to get back to work. There is a great pride every day the uniform is worn and you put yourself through a personal inspection to look good. It may not always be at this level but that pride feeling should never go away with the wearing of the uniform and performing.

Beware of other Officers that might have been released to the street and have an attitude. These Officers may still also be on probation but have an attitude already against people and the system. Stay away from those attitudes. You still have to work with those types of Officers but do not have to think the way they do. They have an attitude because they want it to seem like they have already experienced all that there is to experience and make it seem as if they are veteran Officers. They are already gaining weight and not staying fit, and the new uniform they are wearing is not as sharp as it should be for a new Officer. The Officers spread their negativity to newer Officers like a disease. Remember, this is a career you chose, so be strong and don't listen to these types. Be that "Quiet professional" that we talked about earlier on. You said you wanted to be a professional American police officer, here's your chance. Those loud mouth know-it-alls, can leave police work if they are so unhappy. It may still happen anyway. During the first year in Indiana, police officers are "At-will" employees. They will still be evaluated by a supervisor on a monthly basis and can be fired for anything during the first year. Unfortunately if the supervisor is truly very busy, he may only get to evaluate from reading the new Officers' reports. Reports are not difficult and are easy to evaluate.

If the new Officer is not enjoying the job and does not look forward to coming to work, this may not have been the job that was meant for them. Most of the time this does not occur but the new Officer should be honest with himself and look for another profession and free up this spot for somebody who would also like to give police work a try. No hard feelings, this job/career just isn't for everybody. Reputation developing continues in this stage of the first year and is probably the most important part of it since this is a building year. There are Officers that have developed a negative reputation early on and it has stayed with them throughout their careers. During this first year especially, the Officer should enjoy the job so much that the shift should fly by quickly.

Most new Officers do a decent job of keeping physically fit in this first year but have to be careful of the available food on the beat. There are fast food restaurants out there that work well for getting food if you are running a busy beat. The problem is fast food is very high in fat and carbohydrates and is the cause of many a large Officer along with lack of personal fitness. These restaurants will also discount an Officer's food many a time without them knowing it. It's controversial to accept discounted or free food, and if you are uncomfortable, pay for it. That is a decision that you and only you will have to make. The discounted or free food is for a reason, they may be thanking you for your service to their community but they most likely want something from you. Most of the time it's just your uniform presence; however, it may be so they can continue doing something illegal since they have you there. For example, running an illegal gambling machine in the business that you may not even know is illegal. <u>NEVER ask for a discount or expect one.</u> If you don't bring a way to pay for food each day, then borrow money or go hungry. The best advice is to always have the money out and be ready to pay full price for whatever it is that you're getting. Asking for a discount is totally unacceptable, inappropriate, unprofessional, and is comparable with asking for a pay-off.

During the first year, the arrests that the new Officer made during his field training program and a since will be adjudicated. The Officer will have to testify on behalf of the state. This means going to court, sometimes on your day off and sometimes in the morning after you have worked all night.

It can be a burden, but you knew this when you signed up. Remember the Latin words *sua sponte,* which means "of your own accord." You volunteered for this. The good news is that most departments will pay you to go to court on your off time, and sometimes it is time-and-a-half pay. Going to court can be the best part time job available. With that said, the Officer quickly learns that most cases are pleaded out. That means that the defendant takes a plea agreement with the prosecutor/state. This can be frustrating if the Officer feels the system wasn't harsh enough on the offender. This is natural since most police officers are passionate about the job. The State pleas most cases for a couple of reasons. The state wins the case in a guilty plea. It also clears the court docket for more important cases. Lastly, it may save an Officer that has made a questionable arrest. It's difficult to sue an Officer when a person has pleaded guilty to a crime for which he is suing. If the Officer accepts the fact that this person will most likely re-offend and will have his day in court again. As a matter of fact, he will probably have many days in court. If a crime doesn't shock the community and the system, the suspect will not get much if any punishment through the court system. This is especially true in most urban areas, where the court system and jails are very crowded. When an Officer goes to court, he usually sits there until the case is pleaded. Still he will have to testify during his career.

There are many types of hearings but two types of trials: a bench trial and a jury trial. A bench trial is before the judge and when all the evidence is in and testifying done, the judge will make the decision of guilt. A jury trial can consist of either 6 or 12 people. They decide guilt by the concept of "beyond a reasonable doubt." This is very subjective and not very well explained or defined by judges, prosecutors, and defense attorneys. Therefore many a non-guilty verdicts have been made even when evidence proved the contrary. Also all of the jurors have to agree on guilt or innocence. When they can't, the jury is hung and the judge can declare a mistrial or order the jury to deliberate again. It's not the best system but probably the fairest in the world if you're the one that committed the crime.

TESTIFYING IN COURT

Due to the nature of the judicial system and the frustration it can give an Officer; the Officer develops a dislike for court and will do everything to get out of going to court. Testifying in court is an acquired skill. Nobody is good at it right away. It can take years before you learn how to read juries, judges, and defense attorneys. Once again you are continuing your reputation development in this arena. Remember that lawyers have a sub-culture also. The judge, prosecutor, and defense attorney all belong to the same state Bar Association and any local attorney groups. They may also be in the same political party and drink or play cards together. The point is, right or wrong, they talk about cases and the Officer involved in the cases. They know which Officers are sharp and which ones aren't in their investigations. The judges will tell each other which Officers they believe are not being truthful, and they will remember that when dealing with the Officer in their own court.

Attorneys are not always truthful and almost always manipulative. They will use sneaky tactics to attack an Officer's credibility most often due to the fact that his client has a weak case. This is usually done when the Officer is on the stand testifying. The attorney will try to make you explode. If he's not getting the answer he wants, he will try to make you re-phrase it to his liking and advantage. If you've answered the question to the best of your ability, just say so and remain calm. Remain calm even if the attorney starts raising his voice. If you lose it on the stand in a jury trial, the jury will think of you as "one of those out of control cops," and so will the judge. Keep answers on subject and don't exaggerate or offer any more of an explanation. Simply answer the question that was asked and shut up. You may give the defense more ammunition to discredit you. Do not take this questioning personally, in some ways it is a crazy game. The defense attorney really doesn't care if their client is guilty or not, but they do care that you followed the rules.

In many bench trials, the Officer will stand in front of the judge along with the prosecutor, defense attorney, and the defendant. Police officers do not let people get to close to them. They naturally keep a defensive (but not obvious) stance and at least 3 to 6 feet distance from whomever they are speaking. After a while they just do this automatically. A good, experienced defense attorney knows this and will use this to his advantage. During the Officers testimony when being questioned by the attorney, the attorney will move into this space in an attempt to make the Officer uncomfortable and hopefully cause the Officer to mess up while speaking. It usually works. The best way to prepare for this is to watch the attorneys work while you are in court waiting for your case. There's a good chance you will go up against one of them during your career or get deposed by one. Also, don't skip court. The more you testify, the better you get and the judicial system will notice it.

Beware of the defense attorneys that talk to you outside of court about your case. Unfortunately, some young Officers don't know the defense attorney from the prosecutor since court identification may not be required. Make sure you find out who he is and if he wants to speak to you, have the prosecutor with you. He will bring up that casual conversation in court and use it against you if he can. It's his job.

Being prepared when coming to court is also very

important. Officers that work the street have very long subpoena lists. Once again, most cases will be pleaded out. If the Officer is prepared, the defense will most likely ask for a plea bargain. Many Officers will just wait for court and do their best when they get up to testify. Taking time the night before to go over the case report and probable cause (written facts of the case) will definitely help when testifying. Once again, if the Officer gets a good reputation with the courts, it will follow him throughout his career and with cases later that he wants pleaded.

Work with the prosecutor assigned to your case. Like police, there are good and bad prosecutors. It is their job to decide how far a case will go from the decision to prosecute to the decision to plea. Hopefully he will keep you in the loop when doing this. What helps is keeping in contact by returning phone calls and showing up for depositions. If you have a problem with the prosecutor, go to his supervisor if you and he can't resolve it. If the problem is the main prosecutor, vote against him in the next election.

Defense attorneys can not lie in court. However some do anyway while many times the only one telling the truth in court is the police officer. No matter how much pressure is put on you as an Officer, never lie in court. Always hold on to your honor and dignity. You are an honorable American police officer! The judges can usually tell who has lied and who has told the truth. That is why the outcome of a trial is not usually about right and wrong but who the judge or jury believes the most. If a defense attorney tells a blatant lie or is "fraudulent," you can file a complaint on him. It is a cumbersome process and takes time. In Indiana the complaint is made to the Indiana State Supreme Disciplinary Commission. Most states have a complaint filing process, and you can usually find out how to do it by visiting the state bar association web site. Make sure you get a copy of the trial transcripts (electronically and hard copy). Keep a copy for your records and write up the complaint on the official form. If you have a prosecutor or a lawyer friend that's honorable you can trust, they can help you with the verbiage of the complaint. Use caution when doing this. As mentioned earlier, lawyers have their own sub-culture and may not assist you or try to discourage you. Sometimes they will even give the attorney you are complaining about a heads-up before the commission does. Best advice is to keep it simple, do your best, and don't take it personal.

Chapter 7

Basic Police Work

THE POLICE REPORT

POLICE hate paperwork. Luckily most reporting systems are going digital. Some are still on a call-in basis where you can call your reports in to a dictation system and it gets recorded then typed or saved electronically. Even with the advent of reporting getting easier, police still neglect to take reports when they should or when they are requested. Some departments have a policy that when a citizen requests a report, they get one made. As a police officer, your experience will tell you that the report will probably not be investigated since it may not even be a criminal complaint. Still, if you have to argue with a citizen over taking a report, you should probably just take one. It will save a headache later from a complaint. It also shows the citizen that something was done about this event in their life that they felt compelled to call the police. It would be impossible to take reports on every single run and experience will help you give alternatives to a citizen if a report is truly not merited. A report does more than just document a complaint from an individual. It's actually collecting intelligence for later investigations. That person who made the report may end up a suspect in another investigation years later. That report that you didn't want to take may help solve a major crime, especially if that person has only interacted with the police at the time the report was made to you. Major crimes have been solved this way.

DOCUMENTING THE PROBLEM PEOPLE

The uniformed police officer is the best source of information for detectives that are investigating cases. The Officer is the best informant out there. The uniformed police officer that cares about his beat ultimately learns the problem makers on the beat. Very few Officers nationwide have a photographic memory. A good beat Officer has a system he uses to keep the names, nicknames, and any vital information he feels is necessary to remember his "problem children." The nicknames are especially important since that is the name they are known by others on the street. Once again this is where the uniformed Officer has helped solve major crimes. The Officer can keep his own records of names in whatever way he feels comfortable. The brain is limited in remembering everybody, and as a police officer you will meet more people than you can retain. Some Officers simply use an index card system. With computers in the car now, a simple Word or Excel document can be set up, and the information can be organized and saved to a thumb drive after the shift. It's very important to back-up those files when saving electronically. The simple, basic information that should be saved on an individual in a file is but is not limited to:

1. Name
2. Nickname(s)
3. Birthday
4. Social Security Number (if applicable a Driver License or ID number will also work)

5. Address
6. Associates (who was he with)
7. Reason for stop
8. Description, tattoos, scars, etc.
9. Case number or run number

If you get the reputation as a "Go to" Officer when a detective is working a case, then you are working the beat and getting to know your people. That includes getting to know your good people.

SUSPICIOUS ACTIVITY

If there is one area that does not get taught well in the Field Training Program, it's recognizing suspicious activity. This is nobody's fault since departments have to use younger Officers as field training officers that know how to do the job but not fully developed their own skills.

When a dispatcher receives a call that a person is acting suspiciously and they dispatch an Officer on the run, all the Officer gets is the call, the reason for dispatch, and the description/location of the person and area. Basically, on "suspicious activity" calls, the Officer sometimes has to go on little or no information. The Officer can not stop the individual on that information alone. What the Officer can do is slow down and see if he observes anything suspicious. He can also approach the individual and talk to him and develop the suspicion. If the person runs from him as he's walking up to talk, the suspicion is developed. The running from the Officer is one thing the Officer can say was suspicious. Some judges have said that just running is not enough for the Officer to stop him, while some judges say that is suspicious behavior. Nevertheless, a good basic rule with suspicious activity is to observe and be able to articulate around three things that you observed that were suspicious. Things like the suspect shoving his hands into his pocket after seeing you then turning and walking in the opposite direction. If the run was of suspicion of drug dealing and the dispatcher collected good information from the complainant, you have a good stop. All stops are up for debate when it gets to court. Attorneys love to use the fourth amendment to attack the police.

You may observe only one thing suspicious that a person does and then stop him. After you've stopped him, review what you actually saw and you'll realize that you didn't only witness one but several reasons why he should have been stopped. Even witnesses recall things sometimes days after a crime that can help solve them. The same happens with a police officer. As long as you're telling the truth, you'll be fine. Also you may review a stop long after you have released a suspect and realize later what you missed. Don't be upset at yourself since this happens to even the most veteran Officers.

Some things to look for when observing a suspicious individual:

1. Person shoves his hands in pockets
2. Person appears to have put something in his mouth
3. Person quickly walks away from individual or individuals he was with
4. Person sees Officer and changes direction of walk
5. Person will not maintain eye contact when talking to Officer (suspect might be getting ready to run when doing this)
6. Person favors one side of his hip more than the other (holding the hip where a gun may be)
7. Person gives the police an age that is different than birth date (false information such a name, birthday,

usually means the person has a warrant, is on house arrest, or is not supposed to be driving)
8. Person is looking in cars or in house windows
9. Person runs from Officer when he sees the Officer
10. Person looks upward when answering Officer's question (he is searching for an answer, which will be a lie)

There are other observations that only experience can bring, and no secrets are being given away here. These actions have been going on since police work began and are the same all over the world. *Basically, if you can explain why something was out of the ordinary then you have just explained why that person was suspicious and why you stopped him.*

OFFCER SAFETY PAT DOWN

As mentioned before and it will be stressed in training, Officer Safety should start on day one and never end. An Officer Safety pat down is utilized on the street and has led to many good arrests. The pat down consists of the clothing. The purpose is to search for weapons or anything that is "immediately apparent," such as drugs. The weapons or drugs can be seized and an arrest made. The problem comes when an Officer paints every person with the same brush and pats down everybody. *When an Officer goes to court to justify the pat down, he needs to be able to explain or articulate why he was fearful of this individual.* This is a hard case for the Officer to make especially if he just patted the person down out of habit and was truly not in fear of the person. Being a high crime area will not cut it. If nothing was observed suspiciously, just control the person's movements and not let him put hands in pockets. If he keeps trying to put his hands in the pockets, there's the justification for the pat down. The fear of a weapon being in the pocket was the reason.

Trust your "hunch"—even though it can not be used in court. If you feel something isn't right, do the pat down. If you find an illegal weapon or drugs, confiscate it, document the stop in a report, and let the person go. No civil judge (hopefully) is going to look at case where an Officer is sued for taking those items and letting the person go when he realized it was a bad stop. The arrest may not have been able to be made, but the weapon and drugs are off the street. Use that "hunch" to keep alive even if it's inadmissible in court. This is not an endorsement to pat everybody down or violate their rights.

MENTALLY ILL SUBJECTS

Many more mentally ill subjects walk the streets today than in the past. Due to the poorly-ran state institutions that have been closed and the positive progress made in medication, many are allowed to live a somewhat normal life in society. Basically if a person is not a danger to himself or anybody else, they will not be evaluated by a hospital for mental illness. That means there are people out there that have mental issues but don't realize it and should be on medication or seeing a counselor. When this is not done voluntarily and they do become a danger to themselves or someone else, the police may have to step in. This may come as a run where the Officer does the accepted paperwork to get the individual evaluated or it may come as a court order. It's usually due to the person relapsing from refusing to take the medication. It can also be from mixing medications with illegal street narcotics. It's very important to be empathetic since these individuals don't realize what they are doing and paranoia is usually present. In saying that, always expect a violent encounter. Be quick with detaining the person physically. You can always try to calm them later. These are different types of runs since the individual is not a criminal usually, but they may fight harder and meaner than any criminal. If a mentally ill subject does resist you and you get hurt, just realize that their thoughts are spinning in their head and they can not think straight. These are not personal attacks, but don't let that keep you from winning the fight and staying safe. You will run into some of these individuals later after the medication is under control and they will be a totally different, usually pleasant person. The days of putting all individuals that are mentally ill in state-run institutions are long gone. This problem, like many others in police work, will never go away.

STOPPING MULTIPLE SUSPECTS

Most people will stop and be detained when an Officer requests it. There are those runs when multiple individuals or a group of individuals need to be stopped. If an Officer does this and his back-up is not there yet, he need to verbally control and try to watch the entire group until back-up arrives. The Officer should have everybody put their hands on their heads. For some reason, Officers still have individuals put the hands on the car or on a wall. This is not the way they were trained and this unsafe technique has not been taught in any academy over the last twenty years. When the individual's hands are on a car or wall, they have a very strong base to push off of and attack the Officer. They are actually in a stronger position to fight than the Officer is who only is stabilized by two feet. Also when hands are on a car, they are very close to an individual's waist where most weapons are still kept. There is a video documentary that most academies show where prisoners are training to push off a wall and subdue the Officer that had them "assume the position." By the way, if you observe one or more of these individuals drop something before your back-up arrives, act as if you don't see it. If you react, one or all may run and you've lost control and possibly your suspect. Let them think you were too inept to see them drop the item.

If an item is dropped and no Officer observed it, but it is closer to an individual than it is the others, it's known as *constructive possession.* Even though the law allows you as a police officer to make the judgment based on type of run, proximity of item, suspicious activity observed that supports your arrest and shows that the dropped item belonged to this individual; some judges will not find that person guilty. They believe that a person has to have physical possession of the illicit item to be convicted. When dealing with multiple individuals, some Officers have a tendency to tell all that they will go to jail unless the guilty person admits to the item. This usually fails due to the fact that the Officer is accusing the whole group and has not read them their rights. If a person does admit to it, he may win due to the fact he was being accused and admitted to the crime without being read his rights. If it's a group of juveniles, the parents need to be there when being read the rights. If the whole group is arrested, the charges usually get dropped since it's impossible to make the case in court. Not only that but they are not going to tell on their friends in front of other friends. Once again, document, confiscate, and release. There will be another day. Justice Karma will work, and you will arrest the correct individual some other or even on many other days.

VEHICLE SEARCHES

If you arrest a person, and a vehicle is involved, you may

have to tow the car and do an "inventory search" of the vehicle. Some departments have detailed inventory paperwork that has to be filled out documenting any item in the vehicle. Others allow an Officer to notate anything important in his notebook to cover the department should anything be stolen while it's sitting at the contracted tow yard. (Tow yard thefts are very common occurrences.) If anything illegal is found during the inventory search, your suspect can be additionally charged with another crime. For the Officers that are allowed to make only notations in their notebook, it's advisable, if anything illegal is found to also note items that were around it such as old burger wrappers, stray change, or anything to show that the Officer was actually doing an inventory search and not a search for illicit items only. It also shows the defense attorney that the Officer was thorough and his client will probably plea guilty.

If an Officer stops a car for a traffic offense and observes nothing other than the offense, he may write the individual a traffic citation and release him. If he walks up to the car and the individual appears to be shoving something to hide it, the Officer may get the person out of the vehicle, do a safety pat down, and search the immediate area in the vehicle for evidence.

There will be that individual that all Officers stop who is well versed in the law. This is usually due to the fact that he's been in prison and a part of the system for a long time and may be appearing to be legitimate. His driver's license may be good, and since he knows the law, he may even get out of the vehicle voluntarily. You may have also heard anonymously that he has acquired an illegal weapon and is known to be violent. In this scenario, you can not search the car unless he gives you permission, and he won't since he knows the law. You decide, since something doesn't feel right, to look under the front seat. You find an illegal handgun. He can never own a handgun since he's a felon. Still it would be a bad arrest and a bad search. Once again, document, confiscate, and release the person. No waves will be made since he does not want to go back to prison for a long time. This is not advocating illegally searching vehicles. If you believe a gun is in a car and the individual with a violent patterned past may use it on you or someone else, take it. Trust your inner survival instinct even if you can't use it in court.

CONTACT / COVER

On situations when two officers are dispatched to the same call, one Officer (usually the beat Officer) needs to be the *contact Officer.* The other Officer needs to be the *cover Officer.* The contact Officer will confront the problem person and collect the information for whatever decision needs to be made for the best short-term outcome of the problem. The cover Officer needs to watch the contact Officer's back, and if the situation is in a dwelling, he should do a protective sweep. This is where he makes sure by opening unlocked doors and visually checking the dwelling for basic safety for the Officers. If it means totally losing sight of the contact Officer in a violent situation, the cover Officer can stand by and watch the open areas and call for another Officer (or Officers) to help clear the house. One of the first questions the contact Officer should ask the person or persons he talking to is if there are any other people in the dwelling.

DOMESTIC DISTURBANCES

The most common run a police officer will take, and also the type of run that will never go away, is the domestic disturbance. This involves fights between individuals that usually live with each other or have an intimate relationship with each other. Try to coordinate your arrival with you back-up and never park directly on front of the house. Unless it's a scream for help, wait for your back-up to arrive if you are there first. Once inside, separate the individuals (preferably where they cannot make eye contact) and ask them what is the problem and try to calm them. If no law has been broken, one individual will most likely voluntarily leave and the situation naturally will cool itself. The majority of domestic disturbances are handled like that and nothing more will need to be done. Some police officers make the mistake of telling the people that if they return, someone will go to jail. This is a problem if the man kills the wife or vice versa. Officers are trained not to use that phrase since it can conceal domestic violence by both the victim and the suspect. The family dynamic of protecting your abuser will kick in especially if the husband is the bread winner of the family. Be fair, be neutral, be the police, and arrest when you have to when dealing with a domestic disturbance. An arrest may result in a restraining order, which will hopefully keep the arrested subject out of the house. The best part about it is if you get a run back to the house, you can arrest the individual again on the restraining order, and you won't have to return until the court case is over and they fall back in love with each other. The police can not solve a family's problems; however, we can enforce the law and handle situations in a timely manner. The police are there to make sure no violence occurs.

PATROLLING

Early in law enforcement, police patrolled by walking the beat. It is still done but on a much smaller basis. The advantage to this is the community knew their Officer very well and was trusted since they felt he was a part of the community. As the population grew and cities became more urban, response time for police officers became more important with the community. The hope was to get to the run quicker to catch the crime in progress or solve it quicker since the suspects may still have been in the area. Due to that, now patrol is mostly done in cars. The police car has become an office on wheels complete with a computer and a mountain of equipment for policing in the 21st century.

Patrolling is another area where the Officer needs to avoid a pattern. A good rule to follow is to check your beat at the beginning and near the end of your shift. By doing this you can spend the majority of your time proactively patrolling the high crime or hot spots when not taking runs. It's easy to patrol the same pattern every day since police like consistency. Drug dealers learn the Officer's patterns though. If an Officer sets a pattern that he will drive down the same street every day at the same time, they know not to be on the street. They also know the window of opportunity they have before they see that uniformed Officer again. Police use patterns to find criminal behavior. Criminals use patterns of police behavior to implement criminal behavior.

The Officer also needs to get out of the vehicle occasionally to talk to people. This lets the people see that there is a person patrolling their neighborhood—not a just a police car. Sounds crazy but a car is an object. Talking to the people shows a commitment to the community, their safety and your beat.

COMMUNICATING WITH PEOPLE

Everybody, including active police officers, has had a bad experience with another police officer. Usually this was off-duty or before the victim Officer joined law enforcement. The complaint is usually that the Officer was rude and had a terrible attitude. The job will harden anybody but that does not mean that a police officer has to treat everybody like excrement. There is a time to raise your voice and even yell on the job. This is usually when the Officer has to gain control of a situation or is in a dangerous police action. He should be raising his voice then. It's an extension of his command presence and shows that he is there and is in charge until the immediate situation is resolved. A good veteran Officer knows when to turn this on and turn it off. Too many young Officers enter the job and believe they have to treat everybody with the same tone and anger. They actually come across as if they are being inconvenienced by having to do the job they chose. Sometimes they learn after someone files a complaint or after being observed by a supervisor. They also realize that the same person they are belittling may be the only person that may save the Officer one day when he's losing to a resister. Everyone is a potential informant. Most Officers have had people that they've arrested thank them. That is when you know you have balanced out the yelling and talking. Officers can get in trouble for using profanity; however, if it gets a person to drop a weapon and keeps you or him alive, then use it. Use attitude wisely or it will help diminish your character.

Chapter 8

Dealing with Politics and the Media

EVERY organization has external and internal politics. The police department is no different. Smaller departments seem to have more politics than larger ones, but this could be due to the size and closeness of the departmental community. Politics, like prostitution, will be around forever and can steal the motivation away from an officer if he allows it to happen. Officers will get passed over for promotion for reasons of race, gender, and or "the good ol' boy system." Is it fair? Not at all but neither is life in general. You have to remember why you originally took the job and come to terms within yourself to deal with the politics. It is what it is...

> *The daily press is the evil principle of the modern world, and time will only serve to disclose this fact with greater and greater clearness. The capacity of the newspaper for degeneration is sophistically without limit, since it can always sink lower and lower in its choice of readers. At last it will stir up all those dregs of humanity, which no state or government can control.*
>
> —*Soren Kierkegaard*
> *The Last Years: Journals 1853-55*

Media and city leaders can cause your department to overreact to an incident sometimes causing an investigation to be rushed and sloppy. Many times this results in a bad case that may get thrown out in court. This is sometimes referred to as a knee-jerk reaction. For example, recently in a Midwestern city, a five-year-old boy found his dad's unsecured handgun and accidentally shot and killed his four-year-old brother. A very tragic incident for all involved—including the police that responded. The prosecutor filed charges against the father for neglect. While it was neglectful and extremely tragic; something no parent or family should ever have to experience, the truth is more children are killed by drowning, bike accidents, car accidents, and fires every year. Those parents never get locked up and all accidents have a certain amount of neglect attached to them. The media leaves those incidents alone since they didn't involve a firearm. An accident is an accident and is equally tragic when children die.

The media will pick and choose what they want to report. If they don't think the story will sell and raise ratings, then it won't get reported. While there are good and bad reporters, the media in general is not a friend of the police. Yes they will help when a child is missing or to find a dangerous wanted suspect; but, if a police officer messes up, they will be all over it. It is a good idea to leave the talking to the media supervisors. Some larger departments even have a Public Information Officer (PIO). When you speak to the media, they get you on camera and as a result have file footage of you. If you get accused of something, they will pull up that footage, and you may be found guilty in the eyes of the public even if you did not do anything. This again is politics in action. The media is also very good at isolating part of what you say as a sound bite, which gives the public only part of what you had to say and not the point you are making. (i.e. Your words can easily be taken out of context.) There will not be a platform for you to tell the world that they were misinformed by your partial statement. They are the media, and you will not even get a public apology. They may misquote you, which will be how history documents your statement. Many history books are written from newspaper accounts. If the media has always spun stories, it makes one wonder what really happened with major historical events. You should only talk to the media if you are ordered by a superior. Then you have to since you have to follow any lawful order. Also, if you do decide to make a statement to the media or give your personal opinion about something, you are not covered by the protections of the First Amendment. The U.S. Supreme Court held that, "when public employees make statements pursuant to their official duties, the employees are not speaking as citizens for First Amendment purposes, and the Constitution does not insulate their communications from employer discipline." (Garcetti v. Ceballos, 2006) You can be disciplined for saying something that a higher-up did not like.

Some departments will ask if you want your picture to be released to the media. They will usually get a recruit in the academy to sign a release form and tell them, "if you are a good cop and don't get in trouble, you have nothing to worry about." Most recruits sign the form and don't realize what they just did. Once again, if you are accused of something, whether legitimate or not, they will release your photo to the media. This can have damaging effects to the Officer should he be found not guilty and has to return to his beat. He could be stigmatized and falsely complained on for years since he and his face has been advertised as a problem. If the department does not have a release form for you to sign and keeps your photo private, send a written request (keep a copy) to the Chief of Police (or whatever title the head of the department holds) asking them not to release it. It may not be up to you but if you are falsely accused and your department does not back you (due to politics), the fact they released your photo despite your former request not to may help your case.

You will also have to deal with the *crime du jour* or "crime of the day." This day can last for years. Certain crimes will be expected to always be enforced due to the fact the Criminal Justice System has neglected them in the past. An example is domestic violence. Officers in Indiana are required to have 8 hours of mandatory training a year on domestic violence. The discretion has almost been taken away from the police when violence is used in a domestic situation since it's been shown in studies that arrests actually deter the domestic violence from happening again. (Sherman, 1992) Officers will sometimes have a domestic situation where both man and wife have mutually fought each other and injured each other. An honest police officer would arrest both individuals. Prosecutors did not like this practice and asked Officers to pick who they thought was more of a victim and arrest the one involved in the situation. So, if it truly was a mutual fight, which many are, prosecutors want the Officer to lie or go by his gut instinct and make an arrest. Gut instinct is great and you should always trust it, but it can not be used in court. Telling a lie in court is illegal. Politics! Don't lie or compromise your honor for anyone—even the rulers of the city. They won't stand by you if you get into trouble.

There will be citizen groups that will put pressure on the media and city government to get them to produce a desired outcome for the people they represent. In Indianapolis there is a group of African American preachers that call themselves the Concerned Clergy. Most large cities have similar groups. They feel it is their job to protect the African American Community from the police. During the 1990's they would protest if any young African American males were shot by the police—especially if the Officer was white. This group is also politically motivated and usually looking out for their own interests. Many times they are trying to get their face in the media to prove to their congregations that their monetary offerings are not going to waste. Plus they are trying to get more people to join their church, which translates to more money for them. When they support the current ruling party, they are usually silent. This was obvious in Indianapolis when there were three in-custody prisoner deaths involving white Officers and African American suspects. During the 1990's when there was a Republican Mayor, the clergy protested anytime an incident like this happened where a young African American male died during or after a police action. In 1999, for the first time in over 20 years, a Democrat Mayor was elected in Indianapolis. The three in custody deaths occurred during his eight years as Mayor, and the clergy was silent. The Concerned Clergy are not the only group out there—they are just the most vocal. They tend to show up on your police runs. That is fine as long as they don't interfere. If they ask to talk to you as a patrol Officer, call a supervisor or tell them to speak to your Public Information Officer if you do not wish to speak to them. Be polite, be professional, but also be the police!

These groups mentioned are not friendly to the police. One reason is they, especially the media, feel they protect society from the Government and police officers represent the Government. Our system of Government is not based on the police protecting the innocent from the criminals. It's based on protecting the people from the Government. People in college that major in journalism are usually very liberal and police tend to be conservative. That's just the way it is. For example, police have a strong sense of justice and believe in punishment to deter criminals. In other words, you do the crime, you do the time. The media would ask a question such as, "Do the Police tend to target one group of people over another?" They try to get a response such as, "Blacks or Hispanics." The real answer is "yes," police do target or go after one group more than others—we target the criminals. Liberal types believe in programs to help a person that has been arrested and want very little, if any, prison time be applied. Rehabilitation is their goal even though it rarely works. Any junkie or alcoholic will tell you that forced narcotic or alcohol counseling programs from the courts do not work. Some have admitted to being high in these forced meetings and that they agreed to go to keep from getting jail time.

Having a good reputation will help in dealing with these groups. Yes they will accuse you of being racist and if you are an African American you will be called an "Uncle Tom" from time to time. They will think that since you are a white officer, for some reason, you came from wealth and your ancestors owned their ancestors as slaves. If you are an African American you occasionally get accused of "selling out" to the "man." The truth is most police officers (both white and black) are blue collar descendants. Blue collar workers, whether police or not, come from a poorer class of people during the 1800's and did not own slaves. Unless they are from old money, which would be rare, they are descended from farmers and most likely were poor. They are three to four generations away from being illiterate since their great grandfathers did not get to attend school but had to work the fields. As mentioned before, the police department represents the community it serves, so it will reflect the same types of social problems the community experiences. That is why larger departments will occasionally have a problem with race issues.

> *"There are two kinds of people I can't stand in this world; people who are intolerant of other people's cultures, and the Dutch."*
>
> —*Nigel Powers played by Michael Caine in the movie Goldmember* (2002)

Everybody has prejudices and stereotypes. That will always be present due to the way we are raised and the fact that people and cultures are different. As a police officer, you will have to deal with your own beliefs as well as the beliefs of the people you serve. We all have different belief systems and will until the end of time. The power of a good police officer is that he can put aside his personal beliefs and fairly handle the task at hand in dealing with a person no matter what lifestyle he or she lives. It's comparable to enjoying a song. You may really like the song but can't stand the singer due to his different political beliefs and the fact that he uses his band's popularity to impose them on others. Police officers are actually some of the most opened minded individuals in society. They have to be since they deal with every type of person from nearly every culture and handle them nearly the same way every time. For example, police officers handle domestic disturbances more than any other type of run. If they receive a man-on-man gay domestic run, the majority of police officers will handle it the same way as a heterosexual domestic disturbance. You never hear about this type of incident since it's not news worthy but would show that Officers are not truly homophobic no matter what some groups think. Most good things police do never gets noticed or noticed. Remember, you do police work for the good that you can do, not the praise that you potentially may get. Dealing with your own personal beliefs and recognizing them will help you handle these types of incidents when they come along.

As an Officer, you may get frustrated with certain immigrant groups usually due to a language barrier. Remember that most of the people in these groups are very hard working and are looking for a better life. The Federal Government has failed the country in keeping illegal immigration laws from being enforced. Local police deal with the criminal side effects of this much more than Federal Law Enforcement. It can be very frustrating and yes the immigrants should have had to enter the United States legally as others had to in the past. However, it is an issue that you will have to deal with and handle properly. Other than the American Indians, we are all descended from immigrants and have equal worth as human beings. When the police are called, most people want the officers to show up, be professional, do their job, and leave. They really don't care about the race or gender of the Officer—just take care of the problem and then leave.

As a police officer you will understand the feelings of racism and prejudices. People will treat you differently because of the blue, or whatever the color, of the uniform you wear. Also you may be passed over for a promotion if your department feels it has to promote more minorities or females. Don't be mad at the person getting promoted, he or she would be a fool to pass up the extra money that comes with a promotion. Try to change the system or find another way to be happy without participating in the obvious areas of your department that may not give in to a political pressure to pick and choose for appeasement purposes.

References

Garcetti v. Ceballos, 547 U.S. 410 (May 30, 2006)

Sherman, L.W. Policing Domestic Violence: Experiments and Dilemmas. New York: Free Press, 1992, 189-195.

Beyda, K.E. (Producer), Roach, J (Director). (2002). Goldmember. [Motion Picture]. United States: New Line Cinema.

Chapter 9

Handling Critical Incidents

CRITICAL *Incidents* are situations, outside of normal police work, that are serious enough to cause death but can also include any traumatic event. These events can also be traumatic to all officers involved.

As the initial or perhaps reporting officer on a critical incident run, you are the controller of the crime scene until a detective arrives. You will write down a lot of information and monitor who enters the crime scene. As with any other type of investigation, remember the *golden rules* of police work. Safety first, common sense second, and then you do police work. Immediately, after the scene is secured or made safe, yellow police tape should be put around the immediate crime scene. This is also known as the inner perimeter. The outer perimeter will be blocked streets by support officers keeping people and cars from approaching the inner perimeter. It's not very easy, and people do make it to the inner perimeter. *Nobody other than he initial Officers, detectives, and medics should be in the inner perimeter.* That includes supervisors up to the Chief of Police. If they enter the crime scene since they out-rank you, document in your notebook what they do, where they go, and who they are. It's been said that when you enter a crime scene, you contaminate it by bringing stuff into it, and when you leave the crime scene, you take stuff out of it. A crime scene is sacred ground during the investigation. Anybody that was in the crime scene should be documented in your notebook. You will be accountable for that information later.

Information collecting includes getting descriptions of the suspect before witnesses might even be separated. A quickly-broadcasted description of the suspect will get supporting Officers that are driving around patrolling to be on the look out. This is how they will initially be caught if the suspect has fled the scene. Also be sure to advise what type of weapon the suspect is armed with even if there was one left at the scene. As the story progresses there may be more than one suspect.

If you are a supporting Officer, get busy helping the reporting Officer. Nothing is worse than a bunch of cops that show up just to see the action and stand around. If you are the reporting Officer, tell the other Officers what you need. If you are a supporting Officer, ask the reporting Officer what he needs. Immediately, whether it's been asked for or not, separate the witnesses. Witnesses will change their story if they get together and have a connection to the suspect. When they are separated, if they have different stories, it's actually easier for the detective to sift through and find the truth. Once again if a supervisor shows up and puts all the witnesses in a vehicle together (yes this actually happened and the case went down the tubes on a shooting), document it in your notebook. Supervisors are smart to let the Officers do their job unless it violates policy or law. Sometimes an experienced supervisor needs to step in to help, but for the most part the Officer can handle these situations very professionally with no need for supervision. An Officer should have basic information gathered before the detective arrives; however, many Officers will be overwhelmed, which makes the detective a great help. Let the supervisor update the media when it's okay to do so.

While in the crime scene, try not to touch any evidence but note where it was in your notebook. For example, a gun used in the shooting may be on the ground next to the victim. The victim will have medical personnel attending to him even if he's legally dead. If that gun gets moved accidentally, note it and put an Officer near it to keep it from happening again. Obviously if a gun is near a shot suspect, it will have to be moved a little to keep it from being used again. Be diligent and try not to touch it with your hands. Remember that the crime scene is sacred, and the less it's messed with, the less a defense attorney can attack the investigation in court. After handling a few of these, the Officer gets very good at them. Once the detective arrives, he will take over the investigation and the crime scene will be processed. The process will consist of photographing and possibly video, finger printing, diagramming, blood sampling, evidence collection, and body recovery. If you are part of a small department, all these jobs may be yours including the follow-up. Just do your best. You will never process a crime scene perfectly.

Supporting Officers need to deal with victims and victim family members. These people are in crisis mode and their world has just been turned upside down. They need to be talked to empathetically not sympathetically. Empathy is simply understanding that the person is going through a traumatic event and assuring that person they are understood and being heard. Sympathy is actually letting yourself go through the event with the person, which, for a police officer, is not good. If you sympathize with a person, you will allow yourself to be filled with the same emotions that the person in crisis is experiencing. While this might seem appropriate on a human level, you are not doing anyone a long-term favor by sympathizing. In fact, you aren't doing your job by appropriately processing the crime scene and assisting the investigation. You have to remain in control as a police officer so you can help this person. They will usually be out of control and filled with emotions. You, as a police officer need to control your emotions or they will definitely control you. You will hear that again later. Yes, you may reflect on the incident later in private or when talking to a trusted friend. You won't be the first cop that went home and had to deal with a traumatic incident. Whatever way you deal with it (hopefully not by using alcohol or drugs) you need not be ashamed. You are human and unfortunately have to see humans at their worst. If an incident or incidents are invading your thoughts and dreams consistently, don't be afraid to get some help. Most cities have an Employee Assistance Program (EAP) that provides free, confidential counseling. Don't wait until it affects your work or you could be forced into it, and they will share the findings with the police department. Then a decision will be made to see if you are "Fit for Duty." Related to this, World War II veterans in the last 20 years have started to admit how wartime tragedy and death truly affected them. For a long time many of them felt they had to keep this inside since Hollywood portrayed WWII as romantic and the men as unaffected by the duty. Everything will affect you in one way or another, your brain is a sponge and stores everything you see and hear. You will need to use your inner strength and be strong for the people who can't be for themselves due to a terrible life changing experience that has just occurred.

DEADLY FORCE

As a police officer, you have an awesome power. In certain situations, you may be required to use force to kill somebody. Legal terms mandate you use the terminology that you had to use force to stop somebody who is using the same or greater force against you or somebody else. Most of the time, this will be in the form of using your handgun; however, a car may be used or any other object that can cause death. Even though it may have been justified, a departmental policy may prohibit you from using a vehicle in a deadly force situation or even shoot at a driver that is trying to run you over. Most Officers go through their whole career without ever having to experience a "police action shooting." Sometimes it may be called an "Officer involved shooting." While it is a unique experience and one you may never forget, don't wish or hope it happens during your career. There are Officers that come into the job hoping to be involved in a situation like this. That type of Officer probably barely slipped through the psychological part of the screening process. True warriors are neither ashamed nor proud of having to maim or kill someone. It's just a part of the job.

Most departments use a force continuum that allows an Officer to escalate force just above the amount of force that the suspect is using. That is one area that Law Enforcement differs from the Military. If a person is fighting an Officer, he has to show great control and not go overboard by using too much force. Older veteran Officers are very good at controlling a person with force, especially if that Officer has kept himself fit and periodically reviewed his self defense techniques. It's the younger Officer that tends to apply too much force especially after the suspect is subdued. Once you pass the point of controlling a person and apply extra force since you are mad or upset, you begin to punish the person. The police are not allowed to punish anybody. That is what the courts are for. If a police officer punishes a person, he is committing a civil rights violation and can be federally indicted. You will get mad at people and want to punish them, but hopefully your supporting officers will keep you from going overboard. This is a large part of being a professional American police officer. You must be able to change gears and never be out of control. Always expect trouble but once the fight is over, it's over. Also if you see an Officer getting ready to pass the point of no return, take over the prisoner and have the Officer back off and cool down. By doing this, you may have just saved both of your jobs. There's no problem with getting mad, it happens. As a matter of fact anger will help you if you're fighting for your life. Just don't let the emotions control the fight. Use them to help you fight and go home that night. Don't make the suspect a martyr for the media when they decide to crucify you for the beating and make you the bad guy. They will not even care if that person just shot and killed a cop who also may have been your best friend. The beating of the suspect will then overshadow the initial crime that caused it to happen. Politics will get involved and justice may never get served on that suspect for his initial crime. This has happened in many cities. *Control your emotions or they will control you.*

If you are the Officer that has had to use deadly force, it can be very traumatic. After you make the situation safe and cuff the suspect, get on the radio and broadcast that you've been involved in a police action shooting and let them know what you need. You may have been shot and need an ambulance. The suspect needs one. Tend to yourself first and when help arrives, they can tend to the suspect. The suspect has to be tended to whether you or your fellow Officers want to or not. If he is not and dies, it will haunt the investigation later. The Officers involved will have set themselves up for legal action against them due to the emotional factors involved in the situation. Again, the suspect will become a martyr for everybody who feels they have been mistreated by the police.

Very quickly, several Officers and other support units will

arrive on the scene of your involved shooting. You may be very charged up and angry at this individual you just shot and maybe even killed. As difficult as it may seem, this is a time to deep breathe to get calmed down. Control your breathing; understand what your body is doing. You just had a big-time adrenaline dump, you may be shaking, you may have auditory exclusion and you probably have tunnel vision. This is where your breathing exercises and maturity come into play. Do not yell at the suspect or say anything you will regret later. Everything is discoverable in court. Not only that, but you will be an example of calm professionalism when the other Officers arrive. Limit what you say to making sure the scene is secure and everything is safe. You are now involved in your own homicide investigation. Therefore, your statement needs to be limited to a brief story to your supervisor and supporting Officers. Later, you will have to give a formal statement to the assigned detective. Hopefully your police union will have a union lawyer come out to assist you with giving your statement. As a police officer you have rights called the *Garrity Rights* set forth by the U.S. Supreme Court. They must be invoked by the Officer, and it states that the statement the Officer gives may be used for departmental investigation purposes only and not for subsequent criminal investigations. Sounds good on the surface but the rule has been violated by judges and prosecutors in Indianapolis, which has set a bad precedent. Make sure you and your union lawyer go over your department's use of force policy and your statement. Don't embellish or go off on tangents when giving the statement. Treat it as if you are giving testimony in court. Stick to the facts. The fact is, you will probably be very tired when giving the statement and may remember something the next day to add that may help your case. Just inform your union lawyer about this and have him with you when you amend or add anything to your statement.

For hours after the initial deadly force incident, you will be busy giving statements and assisting the lead detective through the investigation. Good detectives will guide you during this process. There may also be a group of Officers in your department or from surrounding communities that will be there to support you during this, usually very stressful, incident. They may have gone through the same situation in the past or just like to help other Officers. They are most often a great group of Officers, know that you will be busy, will make calls for you, and get you food or anything you need. They are a part of the overwhelming experience but very helpful. This will obviously be a long day or night for the Officer involved.

At the end of the initial investigation, the Officer will be sent or taken home. Usually, the Officer is very exhausted. The Officer will go over the incident multiple times in his head to see if he could have done anything differently. He may even have a dream about the incident that night. The next morning, it is very important to try to start a typical day, which is easier said than done. Reading the newspaper and watching the local news should be avoided especially if the incident was controversial. Listening to people that were not there make judgments can add to the stress as well as stall the Officer's healing process if the incident was traumatic. If getting up every day and going to the gym is normal, then it should definitely be done the day after the incident. Things are not the same but try to keep to your routine as much as possible.

When you are involved in a deadly force incident, you are going to be put on a desk job or some type of job that may keep you out of harm's way on the street. This is common practice and is not meant to be a form of punishment. Your case ultimately may be reviewed by the grand jury, and if it's a politically sensitive case, it may be out of your control. The prosecutor controls the grand jury and will guide them the direction he wants them to go. It's politics again. If you did the right, honorable thing, then no matter what the grand jury decides, you have nothing to be ashamed of. You will be second guessed by the media, community, police department, and your fellow police officers. Keep your head up and don't allow any of it to bring you down.

If death is involved and the case goes before the Grand Jury, the Officer will not be released back to duty until the Grand Jury comes back with a finding. Before that happens, he will probably have to see the departmental psychologist. He will also have to take the *Minnesota Multiphasic Personality Inventory* (MMPI or psychological test) again as he did when trying out for the police department. It is a long two- to three-hour test. This information between the Officer and the psychologist can and will be released to the department to make sure that the Officer is mentally ready to return to the street. This does not mean that the Officer will not experience post traumatic stress disorder (PTSD) later. PTSD can show up years later. If the Officer does experience these problems, he needs to get help. If he doesn't do it himself and it starts affecting the job, his supervisor can put him in for a "Fitness for Duty" check. This means he will be physically and mentally evaluated before being allowed to work the street again. If he's not able, he may be medically pensioned off the department and no longer a police officer. He may apply in the future to return but that is another long, cumbersome, and bureaucratic process.

There is no shame in getting help when a stressful incident affects the Officer. Many police officers that have lead professional careers and have done great work have had to seek help. As a police officer you see things consistently over a 20-year period of people being at their absolute worst and doing things to other people (especially the young and elderly) that will affect you. Most people could not handle this type of work and that is why it takes a special person to answer the call.

CHAPTER 10

Dealing with Change

AS with any profession, police officers hate change. The irony is that the only thing consistent in police work is change. Police officers get used to a routine (which can be dangerous) and when something comes along to change this it throws off their world. This can be in the form of being assigned a new beat, a change in the law, a new policy, new supervisors, the fact that your department may have merged with another department, or a change in departmental philosophy. Nevertheless, the way to survive is to accept change and work with it. Or find a way to make the new policy, laws, rules, or situation to work to your benefit.

Police rules, or SOP's, are like laws in the way that they punish everybody for the actions of one. For example, a department may have a take home car program where they allow Officers to drive their car off-duty. All it takes is one Officer to get filmed by the media speeding down the interstate off duty before the department only allows the Officers to drive to and from work only when off duty. The truth is the majority of the Officers follow the traffic laws; however, politics will kick in especially if the department was embarrassed on the evening news, and everybody will have to pay for one's actions. The same thing happens with laws. Actually only a few break all the laws. The rest of us have to pay for their actions. It's politics again and if laws weren't made, law makers would have to prove their not wasting tax payer money some other way.

Change is not always a bad thing. It's frustrating at times but not always bad. It actually is good for a person because it helps them experience and deal with the stress of the change. Police need to be able to adapt since society is changing. In the past, when females started policing, the predominantly male profession was resistant to it. The change ended up being for the better. There are areas of police work where you need a female due to the sensitive nature of the situation. The same goes for men. Female officers have proved themselves, won awards, saved lives, and done everything that a male officer could do. I'm sure somewhere in early police history, a woman Officer has saved a male Officer's life and totally changed the minds of the stereotyping Officers. That would have been a sight to witness.

When an Officer has spent a decent amount of time in one position, he has a tendency to get burnt out. If this happens in the first couple of years of service, he has probably chosen the wrong profession. Sometimes this has to do with boredom. This is where the Officer needs change and may look elsewhere in the department for it. Sometimes being *detailed* (keeping your assignment but working elsewhere for a time period) will help. In doing this the Officer may realize the job he's doing is a lot better than the other area he was detailed. The grass is not always greener. He may have just needed a break and realizes he misses his regular job. This is the group in which many of your long-term street Officers fall. They may complain, but they will enjoy the street and will finish their career there. If an Officer has a bad reputation, he's going to have difficulty getting detailed since the reputation follows one like a shadow. The Officer will have to determine how dark the shadow will be.

Fitness and a positive personal life helps one avoid burnout because it keeps police work from being their whole life. Balance work and life and understand that they both have an effect on each other and your happiness. Fitness just makes one feel better. Friends, especially non-police friends, will keep an Officer in touch with a normal life style. If you have only police friends, it will take over your life. Heaven forbid you have to leave the department for something controversial, those same friends may never talk to you or associate with you again. Keep you personal life positive.

Changes also occur in police work in stages most during your career. One seasoned Officer best sums it up this way:

Looking back over the past 23 years, I am reminded of the different career stages of police work:

FASCINATION STAGE

This is the 1st through the 4th year. For most, it is the first time outside of the middle class comfort zone. I never saw a dead body. New Officers never dealt with a domestic disturbance. Everything is new and exciting. Shows up early for work, buys anything that is black, has Velcro, and says POLICE on it. The new Officer works past their end of shift time just because they love the job and even ride around the district on their days off. They want to be where the action is; enjoy working middle and late shifts. They wonder what made some of the veteran officers so bitter and promises themselves never to be like that.

FRUSTRATION STAGE

This is the 4th thru 8th year. They show up for work maybe five minutes before roll call. The Officer can't wait for the end of the shift because they have part time job waiting for them. He is frustrated because he now realizes what this job really is. A lot feel unappreciated for what they do. They usually hear from the spouse "you spend all your time working and not with me." Still, he is operating in high speed mode most of the time. He then becomes a detective or tries for promotion. He tries to get a day shift job. He also tries out for specialty units and the Field Training Program.

BEEN THERE DONE THAT STAGE

These are the years 8 trough 15. The Officer is at his best! He has survived several administration changes. He knows who he can and can't trust. Understands the legal system, doesn't take court rulings personally. Has learned that you must be able to change gears every once in a while, and has the ability to be a mentor to younger officers. He still has the energy to work long hours.

ACCEPTANCE STAGE

This is the 15th year and beyond. This is an extension of the "Been there done that" stage. Quite often he will have a day shift job with weekends off. He has a lot of experience of how the game is played. These are usually good, seasoned district officers, detectives, or supervisors that are looking toward retirement and staying out of trouble. He accepts the fact that he may not get promoted or transferred. He talks a lot about the good ol' days. Enjoys laughing at, but also admires the energy of, the younger officers. Lastly, he starts wondering if there really is life after police work.

—Officer Joseph Thompson

Change is inevitable, but don't wait until you get so burned out and bitter to make positive change for yourself. By that time you may have developed a negative reputation from being lazy and having a bad attitude, and nobody will want you working with them. Remember you can leave the street (road or uniform car) for change and can always return. The need for uniformed officers in 911 cars will never go away. The street Officer is the most important player in the whole police game. Every other departmental unit should support the uniform Officer. If the department ever needed to cut resources, the only unit the community could not survive without is the uniform street Officers. They will always be the backbone of the department. Everybody had to start in uniform in the municipal police career. In the military it is said that every Marine is a rifleman. Comparable in municipal law enforcement, every Officer is a street Officer. If all hell broke loose on the streets, any Officer, detective, administrator, or any sworn member of the Department should be able to throw on that uniform and go out to the street and revert back to basic police work. If an Officer does not feel they can do this after they leave the streets, they might not have answered the right call.

CHAPTER 11

Living Off-Duty

POLICING YOUR NEIGHBORHOOD

IT is said that once you become the police, you are always on duty. This is partially true due to the fact that your police powers are vested to you by the state. Police powers don't cease to exist just because you are off-duty or sleeping. However, common sense should prevail when and if using police powers off-duty. For the most part, policing your own neighborhood should be avoided. The neighbors will start knocking on your door when you are sleeping and not use the phone to call the on-duty Officers if you get into the habit of policing your own neighborhood. This does not count for the Officer that receives a free or discounted apartment for proving security to the complex when not at the regular job. That counts as off-duty employment, which is explained later.

Unless you have some secluded property, your neighbors will eventually find out that you are an Officer. They will occasionally ask for advice or complain about a ticket they received. They may even complain about the Officer that wrote them a ticket. Realize when hearing these complaints and answering questions that there are two sides to each story and you were not there when the violation occurred.

Nobody likes being issued a ticket or being arrested so no matter what, and the story is going to be one-sided. Be polite and professional, and let the person know if you would rather not talk about it since you are not working. The word will spread quickly amongst the neighbors, and you may not have to be the local police-complaint outlet anymore.

If there is a neighborhood problem, it's usually going to be a problem family in a problem house. There is usually one of these in every neighborhood, at least temporarily. This house, most likely a rental, always has a lot of people trafficking in and out. There may be limited drug use and dealing. They don't respect the neighborhood and never take care of the house or landscape. The parties are loud coming out of this place. The house may be a rental and the neighborhood association might ignore the overall problem. People and the residents of the house speed through the neighborhood. Naturally, this doesn't happen when they see a marked police car traveling through the neighborhood. As a police officer you know something is going on but it's your neighborhood and you should allow your fellow Officers (not you) to do their job. The neighbors will come to you since the police can not be everywhere at once, and you are the closest one. Still the problem house needs the attention of the police. If it appears that nothing is being done, the neighbors will seek advice again and again. You may even be personally frustrated at the problem. Maybe the beat Officer that runs the beat you live in is lazy. Perhaps everything has been done that could be done, but the problem is still there and yet you were told not to police your own neighborhood.

As an off-duty Officer you should document the problem with your department. This will probably be in the form of a memo to the Chief. Be very detailed in describing the problem. For example, if there are children in the neighborhood and these people are speeding through the neighborhood, the likelihood of a child getting hit by a car is high. Basically, you are making your case for when you have to take police action in your own neighborhood since you are witnessing the law breaking and infractions affecting the quality of life. Also, when you go back to work, give those problem houses on your beat a little more attention.

Note: Police officers have made the verbal mistake of telling people that live around these problem houses that they should think about moving away. Not only is that an inappropriate and offensive statement, but if the Officer truly feels that way about his beat and has no pride, he picked the wrong profession. Nobody wants to be told they should move away from the problem in their own neighborhood!

SOCIAL ACTIVITY

Many departments allow the Officers to take home the police car when off-duty. This is a good program that can benefit everybody. The vehicle isn't run 24 hours a day; thus, extending the life of the car. The car is kept cleaner since the Officer takes personal pride in it and feels a sense of ownership. It benefits the community by increasing police omnipresence. People see more police on the street even when it is an off-duty Officer. A parked police car in a neighborhood where the Officer lives may have a deterrent effect on crime. It's easier sometimes for an Officer to find off-duty employment when they have a marked police car. Officers may have to pay a small portion of the gas proceeds, but it is still a good deal for everyone.

If an Officer plans on drinking alcoholic beverages, the police vehicle should stay parked at home. An Officer getting arrested for DUI in his take-home car may ruin the program for everybody. Some departments have gone to a restricted policy of only allowing the take-home vehicle to be driven to and from work when off-duty. This is not only due to abuse but may also be to the high gas prices.

One thing that looks very bad is, as mentioned earlier, an off-duty Officer speeding in his marked police car. It does happen and is usually given away by the baseball cap that the Officer wears off-duty. Another situation could be if and Officer passes a stranded motorist when off-duty and does not stop to assist. If you don't want to do police work, leave that car at home. When you pull up on an accident you may have to act, and there go your social plans. Not that you wouldn't help anyways if it were an injury accident but just a property damage accident usually doesn't require any more attention than they will get when the reporting Officer arrives.

By driving that marked car off-duty, you are advertising that you are the police, so be prepared to do police work if you are in that position. Having your family in the car may potentially put them in a situation where they may be witnesses or subject to danger should a police action happen. Nevertheless, your mind should be in police mode when driving that car. Talk to your family about what you want them to do if something serious happens. Show them how to use your police radio, and take nothing for granted. Have a plan and practice it. It's easy to say, "Well I just don't do any police work off duty;" however, you may not have a choice. It may be dropped right into your lap! When the pigeons come home to roost, will you be ready? Also your clothing should allow you to be the police if the need arises. That means strong, clean clothing should be worn. Sandals and flip flops should be avoided as they do not support your base very well should you need to get physical. Plus if somebody pulls up and you need assistance, you don't want them to think you are the suspect since you are dressed badly and the real suspect may be more professionally clothed.

As an Officer, you will acquire hats and t-shirts that tell the world you are the police or are affiliated with law enforcement. Some of these will be given to you from departmental and community events. Pride in the job is fabulous and expected; however, these shirts are best for wearing to training and working around the house. They are, unfortunately, a big bulls-eye should you be the victim of an armed robbery when you are out in society. You may not even know the establishment you are in is being robbed before you are shot since you are a perceived threat. Whether off-duty or on-duty, as a warrior you should try to maintain a tactical advantage in the event you have to engage in combat. This is another part of being that silent professional.

Having a social life outside the police department is very healthy. Hopefully, it will involve non-police friends. Some Officers, when asked for identification to enter a drinking establishment will show their badge and department credentials. Once again there is nothing wrong for being proud to be a member of one of the greatest professions. However, when this is done, it has now told the establishment that there is a cop on the premises. Who do you think they are going to go to if they have a problem? Yes, that Officer that may be enjoying his social partaking of alcoholic beverages. Being even a little under the influence and having to take police action doesn't always lead to good decisions being made by the Officer. If he has to use deadly force, there may be a considerable problem later that he was under the influence of alcohol when he had to make a very serious decision. He is going to be second guessed by everybody and their brother anyway. This adds one more major hurdle to coming out of it positively. If an Officer is going to drink off-duty, the gun should stay at home and the badge and credentials should stay hidden. Keep the badge and identification in another pocket, or buy a wallet that conceals the badge and identification. They do make them. Sometimes it's good just to be a good witness. You may actually be the deciding factor in a case later by being a good witness. The fact that you watched instead of acting shows you used good judgment, which can go a long way in court and in your the career.

TRAVELING

Up until recently, and depending on the state to which you are traveling, you could not take your handgun with you. In July 2004, President George W. Bush signed H.R. 218 "The Law Enforcement Officer's Safety Act." This allows Officers to take their handguns out of their state when traveling. It also allows retired Officers to do the same as long as they qualify yearly with the handgun. This is a positive law and helps make Officers feel safer when traveling. In relation to this, should you as a police officer get pulled over, put both of your hands on the wheel. Immediately tell the uniformed Officer that pulled you over that you are an Officer with a gun in the car and tell him where it's located then ask him what he wants you to do. Don't be offended if he secures the gun and holds it until he confirms everything you are saying. He does not know you. *Also no matter who you are, or what rank you hold, when a uniformed Officer arrives on any scene, he is the boss.* If he tells you to get face down on the pavement, do it. Even if you are flashing a badge, do as he says. It may keep you from being shot or killed.

Even though it is legal to carry your gun state to state, you can not take it on an airline unless it is justified for official business. You will be arrested if your handgun is on you or in your luggage. There are police officers all over the country that have been arrested for this. If you feel unarmed when you fly, there are things you can do. Writing pens such as the *Zebra*® brand are very strong and make great stabbing weapons. You can carry them on flight and they make great on-duty weapons as well. A pen will be in your hand more than your gun, and it's even more accessible if you are in a deadly force hand-to-hand encounter. As explained earlier about hand-to-hand combat, think of it as hard on soft and soft on hard time. In a deadly force situation, hard pen inserts into soft eye. Also spray perfumes are less than an ounce of liquid and full of eye-burning alcohol. Spray the eyes with it. Use the hard laptop you brought as a striking device. A tightly rolled up magazine makes a great, short club. Use your imagination, weapons are everywhere and remember that goes for the bad guy too. Once you get control of the suspect, secure the arrest with your belt, and tie his hands behind the back.

OFF-DUTY EMPLOYMENT

Moonlighting, part-time, extra duty, and off-duty employment are just some other ways of saying that police powers are being used to make extra money while not being paid by the government. A private business will hire a police officer to work, usually for cash, as long as he's in uniform and show's a uniform presence. A police car helps since it provides even more of an expanded presence. The Officer may or may not have to fill out a permit, with his department, to work off-duty. The department may also limit the number of hours that they allow the Officer to work. In the past some Officers have made off-duty employment more important than the actual "bread and butter" job they go to every day. The department may also deny off-duty work in a place of ill repute such as a liquor establishment, tavern, problem business, any place, or for any person where it may appear as a conflict of interest. An example of this could be doing private investigation work for a defense attorney.

There will usually be an Officer that schedules the off-duty employment for the private employer. He will ask other Officers that are reliable (your reputation will follow you here also) to work, and he will receive a small cut of each Officer's hourly wage as a scheduling fee.

Officers may be paid in cash on the night they do the work or may get a check later. The business usually offers no benefits or workmen's compensation if the Officer gets hurt while working. The Officer should find out if his department will cover him if injured while working off-duty. The department might not pay the Officer for attending court from any arrests he as to make resulting from Off-duty employment.

If the department allows, Officers will work taverns that truly need a police presence. Since it's an establishment where the goal is to consume alcohol and have fun, trouble usually happens—especially if the place is popular. Taverns need Officers since they will quell problems and keep the on-duty Officers from needing to show up. If a place that serves alcohol receives too many police runs, the local liquor board could revoke the businesses liquor license, which will ultimately put the place out of business. Good people own, run, and work at taverns but so do people with no honor that are either covering up their own criminal activity, are in love with the dollar, and do not care who they use to make it. These are the people that believe that you are their personal police officer while you are working for them and feel they can tell you when you can and cannot arrest somebody in their establishment. They usually have bouncers working that are heavy handed and have been allowed to be that way by other Officers in the past. When an Officer works a tavern for the first time, he needs to tell the owner or manager and the bouncers that he, the Officer, will decide who goes to jail and will not tolerate any abuse by the staff on an unruly customer. If he lays out the law early on, the Officer can control the situation even easier should he have to take a police action. This also helps later when another Officer works for the business.

The other side of this is the Officer that does absolutely nothing. For example, if a fight breaks out in a bar, the bouncers may bring the two fighters outside and send them on their way. Both of them may want the other arrested. Most of the time, the Officer will tell them to go home and sleep it off; and if they still want to file charges, they can do it themselves, usually at the local prosecutor's office. The Officer would not be wrong here but should at least document the incident in a police report. The fighters may meet up later and continue. Or worse, if one of the two should end up dead, a detective will go back to look up the original fight to see what that Officer did or did not do. Merely documenting the fight may actually solve the case.

> *A police report is the best way to keep an Officer out of trouble if no arrest is warranted at the time. This is for both on-duty and off-duty employment. Also, police reports are great archived sources of information for detectives later on when researching suspects and victims in other cases. You can never go wrong by making a police report! It shows the Officer did something about an incident and that he did not ignore the situation.*

As difficult as it may be, the Officer should never allow himself to get into a situation where he has to work off-duty. Extra money should go to a second retirement fund. He should use that money for his hobby, or recreational things such as vacations. Off-duty work is not guaranteed if a department decides to not allow its Officers to work. Some departments put it in the contract to allow Officers to work a certain amount of off-duty work. Off-duty employment does help the department as it keeps the street Officers working the street and not having to respond to runs at a certain place since an Officer is already there.

A common response from police officers regarding extra employment is, "When the department pays me enough, I'll stop working part time." That's a little difficult to believe since police are blue collar workers and there aren't that many people, blue collar or not, that believe they make enough money doing what they are doing. Also, some of these Officers are the types that are never happy. Hypothetically, they are the type that if given a million dollars in cash with no strings attached, they would complain about the denominations in which it was given.

Off-duty employment, much like other aspects of policing, can be positive as long as it's not abused and the Officer remembers he is the police first and being employed privately second. If the private employer is not honorable, then neither is his business. The Officer may not know this going into the extra job but should find other means of off-duty employment elsewhere if he should discover this.

DREAMS

It is very common to dream about your job. After all, it's what you do, and it's a large part of your life. The dreams will range from an actual situation you were involved in, such as a police action shooting, to just about anything whether it has happened to you on the job or not. One common dream police have is being involved in a police action shooting and either the rounds are not stopping the suspect or they arc after leaving your gun and drop right before they would hit the suspect. These dreams are natural and healthy. Your mind is actually training itself in a way by rehearsing situations. Don't let the dreams shock you and realize that many,

many police have and still do experience the same dreams. If you are having a dream that is having a negative affect on you by waking you up and not allowing you to get back to sleep, you may need to talk to a doctor. Remember, that you need rest and fitness to stay on your game and be safe on the streets.

Chapter 12

Those Corrupt Cops!

WHEN speaking of corruption, one tends to think of a uniformed Officer collecting a bag or envelope of money from a small business owner in a back room of that small business. While that may have been true and even common 40 to 50 years back, it hardly exists if at all on the uniform level anymore. This may be due to the fact that police officers are better educated now. They not only receive a good education from a college or the military, but many of the police academies now are top notch and cutting edge. Many of them are considered to be a mixture of military and college. Another reason police are less corrupt is due to the fact that they are paid better than the Officers of past. Decades ago when an Officer answered the call, they usually had a stay-at-home wife and a bundle of kids. They did not make a lot of money, so they had to moonlight and the street pay-off was just too tempting. Officers even had to buy their own guns. They probably were not cheap. Also, even in the past, there were honorable Officers that just plain refused to participate in the pay-off program. Honor has been around forever.

Corruption, like the media and prostitution, will always exist. The uniform level is where it's made an example. The uniform Officer is the most visible representative of the police department. When a department catches an Officer, especially a uniform Officer, at a low rank level doing something corrupt, they will make an example of him. Uniform Officers are like the red-shirted Officers in the old *Star Trek* series. They will be the first to go! Admittedly, an upper-level rank may get caught doing something wrong but it's the blue-shirted patrolman that will usually get caught.

People always accuse police of a so called "Code of Silence." While once again that may have existed in the past, it's just not common on a large scale. Police will find a way to get rid of a dirty cop. It's easy as a police officer to assume that another cop is dirty, but proving it is a different story. First of all, you can't use your hunch to complain on somebody. If you are wrong, you may never shake that stigma. Secondly, the Federal Bureau of Investigation (FBI) investigates Official Misconduct (public corruption) and will not touch a case unless it's a sure thing. They are too busy. Lastly, police tell on each other. They find anonymous ways of doing this, and they will rid the department of that dirty cop. The police officer that screams "rat" the loudest is probably the one that has brought the dirty cop to the surface and is getting something done about it. If a group of Officers get in trouble, one or all of them will always talk. There's a saying that, "The first one on the train gets the best seat." This means that if they talk early about what everybody has done, the system will be easier on them whether criminal or administrative. Somebody will always talk which is another reason to not get involved in corruption and or with corrupt individuals.

Corruption is most common among the upper ranks. This does not mean that there are not honorable people holding the highest positions in the police department. Many of them are long-time police officers that are looking out for the best interest of the department and community and are still honorable. The upper ranks that cover up off-duty misconduct of the other upper ranks are more common. They may do this as to not make the current administration, of which they are part, look bad. It also goes back to politics. Whatever party is in control puts the administrators in place and doesn't want anybody on their watch to be corrupt and ruin chances of staying in power after the next election. The local prosecutor may also be involved in this by using a grand jury to investigate. If it's too politically sensitive, he can refuse to do anything with it and under the confidentiality of a grand jury investigation, he can bury the case forever.

When corrupted, these upper levels of the police department and government officials are not honorable. Part of the honor code is justice, which they swore to uphold. The fact that they are being dishonorable while being part of the justice system is even more unacceptable. As mentioned earlier, corruption will always exist; however, if individual Officers keep their honor and decide not to be that person, corruption will greatly diminish. Hopefully even the upper ranks will be cleansed.

As previously mentioned, police are a reflection of the community. There will always be criminals that make their way into law enforcement. Criminals are opportunists. The police officers that commit crimes, especially on-duty, use police work to open more opportunities for them while still under the protection of the law. They are extra dangerous since they are even more educated about the law than jail house lawyers (prisoners educated in jail about law) and will get around the law by lying and other dishonorable techniques. These criminals have no hint of an honor code and never will. They are simply criminals with a badge and it's unfortunate they may pull a good police officer down with them since they do not care about anybody but themselves. It is also unfortunate that since people are prejudice by nature, they will judge the entire profession by the actions of one bad criminal in uniform. Criminals in uniform are good at not getting discovered; however, they ultimately do. When they do, they have usually said good bye to any friends they thought they had in the police profession. They have disgraced the uniform and traded it for a prison uniform. They are no more than a thug with a badge. Good riddance!

CHAPTER 13

Leaving the Department

ULTIMATELY there will come a time when you have to leave the police department. Hopefully it will be voluntarily. Officers leave for a variety of reasons.

CAREER CHANGE

Some Officers use municipal law enforcement as a stepping stone to Federal law enforcement. These are college graduates or Officers with law degrees that further their career with the Federal government. Many leave to go to the FBI; Drug Enforcement Agency (DEA); and the Bureau of Alcohol, Tobacco, and Firearms (BATF). These aren't the only agencies but are the most popular to join. Since 9/11, the Department of Homeland Security (DHS) has been a popular place to join and so has the Transportation Security Administration (TSA). With the TSA, Officers can become a police on a plane or better known as an Air Marshal.

If the Officer keeps an open mind when entering federal law enforcement, he will do very well. One thing he may not be able to get used to is no longer having the power to stop a speeder or arrest an unruly person for being drunk or disorderly. All the misdemeanor state charges are for state law enforcement. Officers who have left municipal law enforcement have found this frustrating at times. However, they gain the might of the Federal government with better resources and more money to do very complete and thorough investigations. These same Officers have an advantage over many new college graduates, lawyers, and accountants that hires on with them. They bring real street experience, complete with instincts and decent interviewing techniques. They have a skill for reading people that some of their colleagues may never develop. They still have to deal with politics and other people that are less experienced getting promoted because they are connected to a powerful politician or other government employee. It's a similar experience to municipal law enforcement but on a Federal scale with a suit instead of a uniform.

There is a split between Federal and municipal law enforcement. This can be due to the fact that agencies like the FBI will investigate municipal or state police for federal and civil rights violations. Most police officers will say that DEA agents are closest to municipal police since they spend time working the streets and tend to develop the same attitudes towards criminals. The "Feds" offer decent pensions, and you can collect after 20 years of service. Many municipal pensions are vested at 20 years but the Officer can not collect until he is 52 years old. Also the municipal pension can be maxed out at 32 years. If the Officer leaves at 20 years he's locked in and will get a certain percentage (usually one half) of the current patrolman yearly wage. At 32 years, he stops contributing to the pension and will make the most he can from that city's mandated pension. (This is based in the current Indiana pension, which is similar to other cities in other states and maxed out around 75% of a patrolman's yearly wage). The 20-and-out pension is good since the Office or agent is still young enough to start a second career. Federal Law Enforcement retirees tend to land higher paying jobs than municipal law enforcement retirees do. This may be due to the college degree required to go Federal, or it may be the status of having worked for a popular agency like the FBI. Are they better investigators than the municipal Officer? Probably not, but employers think it adds to a business's credibility to have a "G-man" rather than a local Police man or woman.

Officers sometimes decide to leave for a non-law enforcement job. Here's an account of an Officer that left and then came back:

> After eight years in police work, I decided to listen to older, bitter Officers and leave the job. They had told me that there was no money in police work and that I would be much happier making more money in another job. I left and took a job in a foundry where I made more money. After being on this new job a while, I realized there was something missing in my life. I found out that more money did not make me happy, and I had never stopped feeling as if I were somehow still a police officer. I realized that the same older, bitter Officers that told me to leave the job did not follow their own advice and were still working as police officers. The new job was more money but it was also long hours and very boring. The fact that I had a strong faith helped me through this period of my life.
>
> I spent eight years in the foundry and realized that I was very unhappy and not doing what I had been called to do—being a police officer. I decided to go back into police work and even had to go back through the police academy a second time. That alone will usually keep former police officers from entering back into the profession. I still enjoyed the academy on the second tour.

When law enforcement is your calling, follow your heart. After becoming a police officer, adjust the life style around the police income.

Officer John Bolin
Indiana Gaming Commission

LATERAL MOVE

After an Officer has worked on a department for a number of years, and if he's not too old, he may choose to take a job with another police department. He may go for many reasons such as more money. If he's leaving a small department and going to a larger one, it may be for more opportunity and action. He may decide to down size and go to a smaller department or community for less action. Or it could be for personal reasons. Nevertheless, the Officer needs to make sure that he's doing this for the right reasons. If an Officer leaves his department for another one, he usually finds that he is still not happy at his new job. The problems at the new department might be the same as in the old department or they might be different. That said, there are usually problems at every department. Many times the Officer realizes that he had it better at his former department and maybe things weren't so bad. Getting back on his former department may be difficult to impossible. It does happen, but when one leaves a place where one has invested a lot of time and taxpayer money, he may not be welcomed back. Don't leave upset and thoroughly research the new department by riding with a uniformed officer. You'll find out real fast the problems on that department, and it may not be the utopia of which you hoped. Police officers from Australia, Canada, England, and the United States informally gripe about the same issues (mostly internal politics). The grass is not always greener.

RETIREMENT

The day will ultimately come when you have to retire. In Indiana you will be forced out at age 72 if you decide to stay that long. Most Officers don't. Many of them leave before or around age 65. They will most likely leave around age 52 since they have the financial security of pension. Retired Officers will tell you to have a plan before you retire. Very few simply retire and stop working all together. Sure there is a vacation period where the retired Officer relaxes and gets used to his new life but that only lasts so long. Usually he has to go to work just to quell boredom and not get caught in a sedentary life style. Some of them may go back into police work. Retiring to Florida and working in an elderly community is a good pace for the retired Officer. It also helps that the department is hiring more mature Officers who have already been trained to work with the aged community.

Retired Officers are not only libraries of information, but they also have some great advice. For example, start an alternate retirement fund when you start the job as a rookie. There are many investment companies you can do this through, or you can hire a financial planner for a fee who can help you get started with a mutual fund that, by the time you retire, should have a plethora of money in it due to compound interest. By the time you retire, healthcare eats up a lot of the pension. Retiree's insurance usually isn't the best program, and Medicare can not be collected until age 65.

Retired Officers will also tell you to have a plan to retire. Don't just retire cold turkey. This make it a lot easier to go on that vacation, or landscape the yard and fix the house before going on to other employment. Also, if a person tells you to come to them for a job when you retire, make sure it's a sure thing. A common theme is people promising jobs to

Officers after they retire then not fulfilling the promise. This is usually a weak verbal agreement. Remember that after you retire, some people have no need for you anymore since you will not be the police. This also includes so-called friends. There's a saying that, "Retired cops are a dime a dozen." That's somewhat true and if employment is not secured before the Officer leaves the force, retirement my not be the bliss which the Officer had hoped. Have a plan.

Finally, many retired Officers will tell you try not to leave the department angry. This is easier said than done when an Officer has dealt with bureaucracy, politics, and overall negativity throughout his career. Still, if he finishes the career remembering the good things and good friends he has made through the years, he'll end it like he started it, happy or a least not angry.

Just because you've retired does not mean you've stop being a warrior. You are now just a warrior enjoying retirement. Retired Officers never lose their instincts!

MEDICAL PENSION

A medical pension can actually occur anytime in your career. It can be used for physical or even a mental illness. It can be given for an on-duty or off-duty injury. Basically if the Officer can not do the job for health reasons, he may receive a medical pension. The decision usually comes as a recommendation to the department's pension board. It can be appealed later if the Officer feels he can return and do the job or if the department finds you doing police work in another state.

Disappointingly, medical pensions have been abused. Some Officers that want a career change will be "injured" in the line of duty—usually a lower back or neck injury. Those are the two that are difficult for a doctor to prove fraudulent since they consist of mostly pain. The Officer that does this wants the money when he leaves the job. If the Officers reputation is terrible, the department may act like they believe him and send him on his way just to get him off the force.

If an Officer is getting medically pensioned and he does not want to, he may have to hire an attorney. Trying to come back after being medically pensioned is a long process, but it can be done. If being released was due to a physical injury, the Officer may have to research other cities and states and find where a person with a similar injury was allowed to work. Boards, like a court of law, will usually follow precedent, which can work for or against an Officer. Precedent makes it easier for a board to make a decision since it has actually already been made by another board.

Being medically pensioned does not mean the Officer can not go on to other employment. Police department physical requirements are higher than most occupations. The Officer can go on to other physical type employment and have no problem at all. He might even make more money at that job.

DISMISSAL

Being dismissed from a police department can either consist of being asked to resign or actually being fired. Whatever the reason, you are no longer employed by the police department and it may not have been voluntarily. Many departments will offer an Officer the option to resign since it not only makes it appear that the Officer left voluntarily but will help him with future employment. It also saves the department time and money since it is a long, expensive process to actually fire a police employee. Finding another job in law enforcement will be difficult if not impossible.

If an Officer was released and it was for something he

did that was not honorable, hopefully he will look at himself and accept what he did wrong. Nevertheless, it is still never too late to develop an honor code and have an honorable career.

Some Officers after being dismissed go on to make decent private investigators. If they do not like to work hard, they will not enjoy this job. They will do background investigations, surveillance, and a lot of following people. It can be a very profitable job, but picking and choosing clients might not be the private investigator's choice. Also he no longer has access to police computers and resources. If he asks an Officer that is still his friend to get him information, the Officer could get into a lot of trouble (possibly criminally). The private sector has many ways via internet businesses and can obtain information that law enforcement may not be able to obtain, but it has to be paid for and sometimes the private investigator will try to save money by having an Officer look up information for him.

If a retired or dismissed Officer calls you for information, talk to a supervisor to make sure it won't be against the law or departmental policy. If asked to get the information discreetly, a red flag should go up and the Officer should once again consult his supervisor. Remember, the person asking you to do this is making a profit and if he pays you for doing this and you were on duty when you looked up the information, you could be charged with Ghost Employment, which is a felony in most states.

INDICTMENT

If you were an Officer that has been arrested, for all practical purposes your career is done. There have been a few Officers that have been fired over being arrested for a misdemeanor and been hired by other police departments, but it is extremely rare. That usually lasts as long as the local media doesn't find out. All it takes is for the first upset person that was given a speeding ticket to run the Officer's name on the internet to find out that he had been in trouble before. After that, a quick call to the media and the Officer's looking for a new job again.

The best advice here is to get a college degree (if you do not already have one) and find a new career. This may even have to involve moving to where you are not well known. If asked later about your past, just keep it brief and admit that you got in trouble. If an employer finds out later that you weren't truthful, you may be unemployed again.

If you are unemployed because you were found guilty of rape, murder, drug dealing, child molestation, or from any pattern of crimes during your tenure as a police officer, you are on your own.

HAVE A PLAN BEFORE YOU LEAVE!

CHAPTER 14

Common Occurrences: Suicide, Divorce, and Alcoholism

SUICIDE

SUICIDES happened more often than people realize. The media rarely report them unless the suicide combined with a homicide. They actually occur mostly among the elderly. The two states with the highest suicide rates are Florida and Arizona. That is due to the fact that many people retire to these states. It is believed that sickness and loneliness are reasons the elderly take their lives.

When one becomes a police officer, they are more likely to commit suicide than being killed in a homicide. An Officer is more likely to shoot and kill himself than have a criminal do it.

What is the difference between a police officer killing himself and the samurai? They are both warriors!

The simple answer is different time, different culture. The samurai culture basically ended around 1850. Even then, they were allowed to do what was termed as *seppuku* or *hara-kiri*. This was allowed many times during the samurai period if the samurai himself had committed an act that would have been punishable by death and was only allowed to the samurai. (Ratti and Westbrook, 1973) Regular citizens were usually put to death by the police or the samurai when they committed an act that was punishable by death. Still, they were also allowed to kill themselves if they were defeated in battle or if their boss had done an unlawful act. Some were allowed to kill themselves if they did something that they felt was not honorable. It didn't happen often, but it did happen and the practice ceased as the samurai culture faded. It returned during World War II, but it was fed to the Japanese people as an alternative to being captured by the Americans; additionally, the kamikaze fighter pilots used suicide. No culture is perfect and neither were the great samurai warriors. Many samurai were married and had children. Even back then, you can not say that the immediate family was not affected by this ritual of suicide. Many times the wife had to become a prostitute to support the family afterwards since there weren't many professions for a woman, and there was no life insurance available.

When a police officer kills himself, it's usually done with a firearm. The firearm is the Officer's tool that he has relied on to keep him alive, and it's readily available. The Officer is usually going to be a white male but suicide does not discriminate. All races and genders of police have committed the act. In one Midwestern city, 33% of the Officers were retired at the time they committed suicide, 93% were male, 86% used a firearm, and 14% hung themselves. Eighty percent of those same suicides involved personal problems such as alcohol, divorce, and health problems. Twenty percent of the suicides were due to possible termination or PSTD. Still there is a lack of sufficient data to fully identify all the issues involved in police suicide. The reason for this is because police do not like to talk about this subject, and the one that can answer questions about the suicide is usually dead from the act (if they were successful).

Suicide, whether done by a police officer or not, is a very selfish act. It has a rippling affect. It initially affects six people but when it's done by a police officer, it affects more since police are a family. Suicide can cause division in the workplace. There is a lot of finger pointing after a police suicide. Many Officers are hurt and mad at the department for not recognizing that the deceased Officer had some issues. Those same Officers need to look at themselves. Despite this, if a person truly wants to kill themselves, there's not much anybody can do. The truth is, most of these Officers probably did not want to kill themselves but could not find a way to ask for help. Some Officers are mad at the individual for killing himself due to religious reasons, and some are angry that the person was selfish and did not care who he hurt by committing the act. Sadly, one thing you can be sure of after entering law enforcement is the fact that you will know one or more police officers that have killed themselves. Whether mad or sad, suicide has a lasting emotional affect on fellow Officers and can kill morale. It happens way too often.

Police work has been coined as the second highest stress producing profession following the job of a miner. There are many ways to combat stress as mentioned earlier. Exercise, good nutrition, and a positive life style helps. However, since it has been found that depression can be inherited, medication may be necessary. If you suspect another Officer that has gone through some major life changes (i.e. divorce, loss of a loved one, police action shooting, any critical incident or a combination) is talking a lot about death but not necessarily his own death, he may be contemplating suicide. Keep an eye out for depression, burn out, violent behavior, or increased alcohol consumption. If the person is acting way out of the ordinary, something is going on in his life. If you think he needs help, get it for him and involve your supervisor. Do not be afraid to ask the Officer if he's thinking about killing himself. You will be asking total strangers in the course of your duty the same question so don't be afraid to ask your co-worker friend. If he actually kills himself, you will wish you could have done something to try to prevent it and at least you can be assured that you tried to do something. Still, once again, if a person truly wants to kill himself, nobody can stop them. As painful as it is for the survivor's to accept, the only person truly responsible for the suicide is the one that commits it. Private counseling is almost always available for free to the police. If you are harboring these thoughts, do yourself and every person you know a favor and talk to a professional.

DIVORCE

Many myths are out there about the police. One of them is that domestic violence is more common among police officers. It does occur as in every single other profession, but it is not more common than any other. Divorce is another occurrence that is said to be higher among police officers. While there are many police web sites that claim this and even police officers that will say it, we just don't know if that's true. There's no study (that the authors could find at the time of this writing) that shows what occupations have higher divorce rates than others. Even so, divorce still happens quite often among the police.

Police work will probably always be a male-dominated profession. There are always temptations in life and women that are attracted to a man in uniform. Additionally, there are men that are attracted to women in uniform too. Police officers meet a lot of people at both regular and off-duty work. Temptations are always going to be there. A non-supportive spouse that has a jealousy problem due to poor self confidence does not help. Dating or living with a person for up to three years can be a smart move if it can be done. The different lifestyle of a police officer is not always easy for a spouse to assimilate to. Some departments have a spouse academy or a support group for police officers and their wives. It shows the spouse that they are not alone, and they have other wives they can speak to and share experiences. Police officers that date a girl for a couple of years or live with them, let their potential spouse know and experience what they are getting into. This helps, but divorce also does not discriminate. Some people just fall out of love and decide that it's time to part ways and move on.

When an Officer does go through a divorce, it's probably very difficult to express what he or she is going through. They may find another Officer that has also been through a divorce but still may feel alone in the world. Cycles of divorce have been compared to losing a loved one. It is the death of a marriage and a loss so the emotions are going to be similar. Elisabeth Kubler-Ross (1997) studied death and loss back in the 1960's. She proved that feelings come in stages such as isolation, anger, bargaining, depression, and acceptance. The danger for police comes in the bargaining and the depression stages. In the bargaining stage they want to make the pain go away, so they may ask God for help or slip into a bottle. Depression is the stage that follows and is also where the Officer should be monitored for possible help should he reach out. As with any loss, the Officer should recognize these stages, which will help to pass through them and eventually get through the last stage of acceptance and move on.

ALCOHOLISM

If alcohol were discovered today, it would be a controlled substance and illegal. In some ways it is controlled by the state and federal government, but you do not need a prescription to get it. Still Jesus drank it, and it's been around ever since primitive people left their grape juice out to spoil and was accidentally drank by the tribe causing them to feel really funny. It is a legal vice, and police are supposed to obey the law. So when it's time to let loose, alcohol becomes a friend.

Most people, including Officers, that drink are socially responsible drinkers. There are those that let alcohol take over their life. The bottle becomes more important than the job and the family. Alcohol is an escape and is a way to deal with stress. It's not a positive way to deal with stress, but it's much easier than exercising plus you can do it around a bunch of police friends and hopefully laugh a lot. Sooner or later though, the problems that you are trying to cover up are still going to be there. If drinking is the only thing that you are doing to handle the problems in your life, it will become an additional problem especially if it's combined with an addictive personality. Alcohol may be the gateway to other problems or the underlying factor to problems.

Drinking on duty about 30 to 40 years back was very common. Rookies were often taken into a bar on the first day and given a shot to calm down. If they refused, it was a little harder to be accepted. Alcohol affects judgment and this is where an Officer needs always have his "A Game." Now some departments will issue an Officer a Portable Breath Test (PBT) to see if he has any alcohol on his breath after shooting somebody. This can change the shooting from justified to criminal.

This is another area where police officers need to police themselves. If an Officer comes to work and it's obvious (usually through smell) that he has been boozing all night, he needs to go home. If you feel it's not your position to confront the Officer, make the supervisor aware and have him do his job. The Officer probably needs some help and now will have to get help or he might have to find another job.

Alcoholism is a sickness, and if you let your employer know that you are doing something like Alcoholics Anonymous to fight it, you're going to be in better shape that after getting in trouble with the law. The department can treat it as an illness, but when the law is broken, they can get rid of you, sick or not. Many alcoholics are in denial, so until they hit rock bottom by getting arrested for driving drunk, they will probably not get any help.

References

Ratti, O. and Westbrook, A. Secrets of the Samurai. Vermont and Tokyo, Japan: Charles E. Tuttle Company, Inc, 1973, 93.

Kubler-Ross, Elisabeth. On Death and Dying. New York: Simon and Shuster, 1997, 63-147.

Chapter 15

Emotional Intelligence

A BALANCING ACT

As a police officer you are going to see, experience, and witness things that will disturb you. As a normal human being you will also have family problems just like any other American family. The trick is to not let one interfere with the other. Both work and personal life will affect each other, but you need to remain in control. The job is not worth losing your family over; however, losing your job because you're letting personal problems interfere is also wrong. It is your responsibility to be an adult and handle your problems in the most sensible and honorable way you can. It is not up to your supervisors to work around your problems. They will help as much as they can but only to a certain extent. There are police officers that never seem to get out of a rut of problems throughout their career. Some of them have learned to work the system and are lucky they haven't been discovered and medically pensioned or even fired.

Bringing problems home is worse than bringing them to work. Policing is a job, and there are other jobs to have. Many times a spouse of a police officer can't deal with the change after the other spouse becomes a police officer. Very quickly an Officer may learn that the spouse is a good listener but will use that same information against him or her in an argument later on when the job becomes an issue. It can be easier on a relationship if a person becomes a police officer before he or she gets married. In this instance, the fiancé at least knows what he or she is getting into being married. The changes in life of becoming an Officer causes many that were already married to have problems ultimately leading to divorce. That does not mean this always happens, but it is very common. As long as any spouse is open-minded, venting to them after a rough day is fine. If they are not open-minded, the Officer closes up and will vent to someone else. The job and home life should be separate so the Officer won't take his work angst out on his family or the bottle.

When Officers first come on to the job they tend to be very passionate about the occupation, which is great. They have chosen a great profession. Sometimes though they let the careers overshadow everything else by keeping and hanging out with their police friends only. They tend to spend a lot of personal money on extra equipment early on and will even max out credit cards. There's nothing wrong with any of this in moderation but their world contains only the police world. As mentioned before, never lose the non-police friends. They will help keep you balanced and help you keep you faith in people to a certain extent. They will never see what you will in your career but nevertheless, a good friend is a good friend. They do not have to be other police officers. If your friend is a police officer and is also bitter and angry for the same reasons you are, he is not going to help you with whatever problem you are dealing with. He is mirroring the same problem. If talking to someone is what you need, use your non-police friends once in a while. Police work will be a large part of your life. Balance your life with positive relationships involving non-police friends. Having a hobby is also very healthy in diverting from police during the off time.

People that become police officers aren't always honest with themselves about emotionally being able to handle the job. A person should look at him or herself in the mirror and be heartfelt and honest as to whether they can pull a trigger and possibly kill somebody. Granted nobody truly knows what that situation is like until they experience it. Still if you are honest with yourself, you will find the answer.

Do you have the emotional intelligence to admit that the job is not for you? There is no shame in realizing after being an officer a few years that it was not the job you thought it would be and that it's time to find other employment. Leave the job and free up the spot for somebody who is waiting. When the economy is bad, the security of a municipal policing job get more attractive to people. If you've been on several years and are too lazy to find another job, you are doing a disservice to the police profession and your fellow workers.

Chapter 16

Terrorism

AMERICANS are resilient people. The ways Americans recover after disasters and come to the aid of people in need are a couple of things that make this country so great. To our fault though, we tend to ignore the obvious, and the police are no different.

Everybody has heard that the world changed after September 11, 2001. Everybody probably believes it to a certain extent yet many act as if September 11th never happened. Or since it was in the past and not happening at this moment, terrorism is considered out of sight out of mind. Even some police officers feel this way. Remember again that police are a reflection of the community, so the denial that another attack is going to happen is also believed among some police. On September 11, 2001, America got caught with its pants down. There were many indicators that have already been gone over by other books and the Federal government that signaled the attacks on that tragic day. We had already forgotten that we had been attacked in this country before by the same radicals, and we did not take it seriously.

Federal Law enforcement shares some of the same problems as local law enforcement—especially the problem of Officers or agents not doing their jobs. A small number do the work for everybody. A few agents did go that extra mile and tried to give their bosses a heads-up on the attacks and were basically ignored due to law enforcement in America being mostly reactive instead of proactive. The Government, on both state and federal levels, had to be awakened by an attack before they would do anything. Both government entities have people sitting in the big seats collecting a large salary (especially for law enforcement), and if they can sit in the big seat and get away with doing very little to nothing, they will do so until an event forces them to work. America was coming out of the 1980's and 1990's, which were two of the most politically correct decades of the 20th century. Police departments and federal law enforcement didn't want to come across as being too aggressive to the community. It was out of balance. Before and after September 11th there were Officers that took these threats seriously enough to research the problem on a local level. Other Officers looked at them like they were crazy even after September 11th! They think that his problem of home-grown and radical Islamist terrorism is just going to go away. Whether you agree with fighting terrorism in a foreign war or not, there is a very good chance we will be attacked again on American soil. There are always going to be groups in America that want to terrorize the government and the American people. The radical Islamists are still upset at us in the West for the crusades that happened about 1000 years ago. Some of the life styles in the Middle East have not even changed since then, so why should the attitude/hate? There are more Muslims in the world than there are Christians. The majority of the Muslims, like Christians, are good, spiritual people that love their neighbor. Just going by numbers, there are many more angry Muslims than angry Christians; however, they both are responsible for terrorist acts in America. They are killing for God, so they believe that it's not a sin and that it's the morally correct action to take. Radical religious terrorists believe they are blessed as a soldier in God's army.

As a police officer, it's difficult to say what suspicious activity to look for in an anticipation of a terrorist act. Before the attack happens, something that's out of the ordinary might be observable. Still it's smart to always anticipate that an attack will happen. The police and the firemen are always the first responders. Around 411 emergency workers died responding on 9/11. Around 60 of the first responders that died were police officers. Municipal police officers need to accept the inevitable and be prepared for another attack. No other attack in American history killed more police officers or firemen at one time. That alone should be enough for any police officer to take this threat seriously.

Police officers die in the line of duty often from letting their guard down. Just because the government lets the country's guard down does not mean that you individually as a police officer have to drop your guard. Keep informed on what's going on in the world since it will affect the local community. Watch what is happening in Israel, and see how Israel is getting along with its neighbors that want to kick Israel out of the neighborhood. America will always be a big brother to Israel. There are biblical and democratic reasons for this and it will most likely always be that way. That alone will always mark America for another attack.

When the attack in America happens, America will rally around the flag for a minute until the anger ceases. Keeping vigilant is not an easy thing to do. After the media advertised young Americans coming home in body bags during the Vietnam War, it seems as if the greatest nation in the world has lost the steam for combat. The war is going to be fought on American soil in the future since going over seas is getting less and less popular with the American people. The uniformed police officer will be a primary target since he is uniformed and that uniform also symbolizes defending liberty and freedom. The uniform might as well be a big, blue, bull's-eye. That is why the uniformed street Officer needs to keep his guard up always for anything that is out of the ordinary. Trust that instinct and follow that hunch.

> *ALWAYS BE PREPARED MENTALLY AND PHYSICALLY. YOU'LL PROBABLY BE RESPONDING TO A HORRIFIC SIGHT. POLICE HAVE TO STAY IN CONTROL WHEN EVERYTHING AND EVERYONE ELSE IS OUT OF CONTROL. WE ARE THE FRONTLINE ON THE WAR ON DOMESTIC TERRORISM.*

Chapter 17

The System

THE criminal justice system is more complex than people realize. Laws that protect us also complicate and bureaucratize situations. It would seem that if the concepts of justice were kept simple, such as, "If you do the crime, you do the time," things would be much easier.

As a police officer there will be community meetings that you will attend. You and your uniform will represent and symbolize the whole criminal justice system. In some cases this can be an unfair bourdon on the Officer. The Officer often times takes a verbal beating from the frustrated and rightly upset community over crime in their neighborhood. The truth is the police officer is there to react and arrest when he can in a timely manner. The arrest is a temporary solution and police administrators want to treat the problem as if it is only a police problem, which they think the department should fix themselves. While that is noble and yes police and their administrators should be accountable, they can only keep arresting the same individuals so many times before the judges have to take some accountability and sentence the law-breaking individuals. That is the simple answer of why the system does not work and why responsibility is placed on the police.

The system as a whole is complicated as mentioned earlier.

Maybe it would take a massive overhaul to fix it, which might be impossible. Every part of the Criminal Justice system indirectly will have an effect on the other parts. On each level, there are a small percentage of people doing the work for everybody else. Admittedly, people have different work ethics but if, in a perfect world, everybody came to work and did what they were supposed to do, there would probably be a positive impact on crime and justice.

In uniformed police work, there are Officers that balance their proactive and reactive work and get things done in a timely manner. Since they are efficient and available, they have to take up the slack for the other Officers that just don't care anymore, which can cause runs to get backed up and response times to grow longer. Delays like this, sometimes unavoidable, cause suspects to get away and evidence to be destroyed. Even though the advent of the automobile initially made response times quicker, higher crime, a larger urban population, fewer police officers, and Officers not doing their jobs have slowed those response times down again. After an Officer makes a righteous arrest, the suspect goes to jail where the case gets a quick look by the prosecutor and judge. If the case is not deemed particularly evil, the suspect may be released on bond or with just a promise to reappear. The suspect may be back into society anywhere from 12 to 36 hours after the arrest. The police have no control over this, but they will take the heat for the subsequent crime this person will commit after he is released.

The crime-committing suspect may also be released since the prosecutor has discretion to drop charges even though there was plenty of probable cause to fully charge the suspect. Sometimes they drop the charges because the Officer made a weak arrest despite temporarily solving the problem at hand. Most prosecutors do their best with what they are given at the time of arrest. The fact is that many times, the initial 12 to 36 hours (based on Indianapolis jail holding times) is the only jail time a suspect may do. Many suspects have committed so many felonies that they are eligible as a Habitual Officer, which usually means mandatory prison time. These cases take a lot of research by the prosecutor to dig up old court convictions, and many do not want to do it since it takes more work than they are willing to give. It may also be due to the fact that they are too busy running cases through that they just don't have time to pursue the habitual cases. If the suspect makes the news and it becomes a politically hot for the elected prosecutor, they will do whatever it takes to bring the rod of justice down on this person.

Judges are under pressure to give lenient sentences since the jails and prisons are overcrowded and the costs for keeping prisoners are constantly rising. Sometimes judges, especially liberal judges, let personal feelings get in the way of the black-and-white law. Justice is supposed to be blind, but it really is not. Street prostitution is a major complaint in every big city. In some cities it's a bigger complaint than street drug dealing, which is a breeding ground for prostitution anyway. After so many convictions for misdemeanor prostitution, it becomes a felony whenever the prostitute gets arrested afterwards. What is a major problem and concern to the community that the police have been handling since the beginning of vice work, many judges feel is not a major crime. Many judges will not even sentence the felons to any time in jail. The counter argument is to legalize prostitution. In Las Vegas where prostitution is legal in the outer counties, illegal street prostitution still exists. These same people that want it legalized think twice when they realize that their neighborhood could become infested with prostitution and the garbage that follows. Furthermore, organized crime always flourishes when vices arrive.

If a person gets out of jail and is put on probation or

parole, they will be assigned a probation or parole officer. They have to report to the officer and they have conditions they have to comply with, or they have to go or go back to jail. If the officer that is supposed to be monitoring this person is overworked or is plain lazy, a violation may not be put on the person. Violating an offender takes a lot of documentation and work that has to go back before the court. Depending on the severity of the violation, the judge may not violate the offender. There are many hard working probation and parole officers and they occasionally will use the police to assist them in a sweep that allows them to search the living area of the individual. This is a very effective tool for the police if they can find a probation officer willing to assist. Like many government jobs, probation and parole departments have a few people supervising many offenders. On top of all that, again, there are a few doing the job for the majority. Some offenders have stated that their probation passed and they only had to meet their officer once and may have spoke via phone afterwards, but that was it.

Tax dollars will never stop being a hot topic for politicians. Prisons are built only when they are absolutely needed. When it gets to this point, they are usually overcrowded. During the 1980's and 1990's there was a big push for rehabilitation—then crack cocaine arrived during the war on drugs. Any junkie will tell you that forced rehabilitation through chemical-dependency counseling does not work if they do not want to stop. Sitting through a counseling session was better than sitting in jail—at least they could be high or intoxicated during the counseling session. Many programs came along, and imprisonment was put on the back burner as a result. Add to that the millions of immigrants that have entered the state illegally, and there is simply not enough room in prison. The states need to build more prisons and utilize new technologies to make them more cost effective and secure. By the time a person gets to prison, it's no longer a deterrent. He has been conditioned by the pampering of the current system that prepares them for the next level instead of making them fear it. Sometimes life in prison is much more structured and better than life on the outside. Going back to prison is a vacation from committing crime.

If government workers on every level of the criminal justice system change their work ethic and decide to come to work and put in an honest days work doing the job, it would be a good start to helping this system. Accountability on every level needs to be the standard and not the exception. Promoting un-qualified people that are not leaders or trained to lead adds to the problem. *Earning* rank gets more respect than *acquiring* rank.

The police can accept only a very small portion of the blame for crime problems. However, they take the brunt of the criticism and blame since they are the most accessible to the public and the uniform is most visible and symbolic of the criminal justice system. It can add to the many negative aspects of the job if the Officer allows it.

Chapter 18

Honor and Your Personal Code Revisited

THE first chapter of this book was the shortest but was the most important. Your training and experience will carry you through the great career of policing, but your mental and physical state will keep you alive. Practicing that personal honor code will help keep you positive and not let the stress eat you up. Part of the reason for this is at the end of your shift you can look in the mirror and know that you've made the best decisions that you could since you based them on honor.

You will still make mistakes throughout your career and again nobody in any job is a saint. Still, you will make fewer and fewer mistakes because you've allowed yourself to develop good character—a common trait of many of the great warriors throughout history. There's nothing radical about being a modern day warrior, you just don't advertise it since humility is a by-product of your code. Being that silent professional speaks louder than any award you or anybody else may receive in your career.

Use what you've read in this book and go out and make the job more honorable. Make the profession a more honorable one since you worked in it. Leave the job a better place than it was when you entered it. Many have died not only in war but on the streets so you could live in this great country. Honor their memories by being the best you can possibly be. Don't tarnish the badge. Be that Professional American Police Officer!

STAY ALERT AND STAY SAFE!